To Diane,
It was so † have our paths
at the WMI Syn.
I hope they cross
soon ~ love in Christ
Holli Jan. 94

# The PMS Puzzle

*Letting God Put The Pieces
In Their Place*

## by
## Holli Kenley

Printed in the United States of America

International Standard Book Number 0-939513-76-5

Published by
Joy Publishing
P.O. Box 827
San Juan Capistrano CA 92675

# Table Of Contents

INTRODUCTION

Introduction ................................. 5
Dedication ................................. 6
Foreword ................................. 7


PIECE ONE: PUT YOUR FEARS TO REST

Questions About PMS ............................ 11
What Is Premenstrual Syndrome? .................... 12


PIECE TWO: ACCEPTING MY OWN PMS

"What's Wrong with Me" ........................... 19
Confusion ................................. 21
Secrets ................................. 25
Desperation ................................. 31
Pain And Shame ................................. 37
Darkness ................................. 41
Craziness ................................. 47
Hope And Help ................................. 55
Hard Work ................................. 63
Darkness Returns ................................. 69
Pieces Of The Puzzle ............................ 79
Free And Faithful ................................. 87
Losing To Win ................................. 95


PIECE THREE: THE JOY OR RECOVERY

Guidelines For Recovery ........................... 107
What Can A Woman Do About PMS? ................. 107
How Will You Know If You Have Found
The Most Effective Treatment Plan? .................. 108
   1.    Diagnosis Of PMS Using The Menstrual Chart . 109

2.    A Diet Plan . . . . . . . . . . . . . . . . . . . . . . . . . . . . 111
3.    The Three Hour Diet . . . . . . . . . . . . . . . . . . . . 117
4.    Vitamin Supplement . . . . . . . . . . . . . . . . . . . 119
5.    Stress Reduction . . . . . . . . . . . . . . . . . . . . . . . 122
6.    Exercise . . . . . . . . . . . . . . . . . . . . . . . . . . . . 125
7.    Rest . . . . . . . . . . . . . . . . . . . . . . . . . . . . . . . 126
8.    Natural Progesterone Therapy . . . . . . . . . . . . 128
9.    Counseling/Support Groups . . . . . . . . . . . . . . 131
How Can I Do All Of This? . . . . . . . . . . . . . . . . . . . . . . . . 133

## PIECE FOUR: HOW OUR PMS AFFECTS THOSE WE LOVE

A Message To The Children Of PMS Sufferers . . . . . . . . . . 137
A Message To The Men In The Lives of PMS Sufferers . . . . 140

## THE FINAL PEACE: A RELATIONSHIP WITH THE LIVING GOD

My Gift From God, My Gift To You . . . . . . . . . . . . . . . . . . . 149
PMS Prayer . . . . . . . . . . . . . . . . . . . . . . . . . . . . . . . 149
Closing . . . . . . . . . . . . . . . . . . . . . . . . . . . . . . . 150

## APPENDIX

About The Author . . . . . . . . . . . . . . . . . . . . . . . . . . . . 152
References And Recommended Readings . . . . . . . . . . . . 155

It is my hope that any woman suffering from PMS will not have to continue that battle needlessly.

Granted, my case was an acute one. However, it is ludicrous for any woman to be robbed of the joy of living, even if it is just for a day or two, or weeks on end.

PMS is not a crutch or an excuse for irrational unacceptable behavior. It is an illness and must be treated as such or it can and will disable a woman, and it can and will erect barriers between a woman and those who love her.

Holli Kenley

To my husband, Dan and to my daughter, Alexis, who, in spite of the PMS, gave to me selflessly and loved me unconditionally.

A heartfelt thank you to each person mentioned in this story—for the courage, the commitment, and the care demonstrated by each one of you.

# FOREWORD

Premenstrual Syndrome—better known as PMS—plagues 60-80% of all women in the world. It is so unfortunate that the majority of women do not seek help. For those that do, many times the professional responds with words such as "Live with it—it too shall pass," or "Since you are a woman, this is part of being you!" More often than not, drugs are used that can be habit forming (which treat the present symptoms and not the cause) and also give negative side effects. It is no wonder why so many suffer silently.

I feel that Holli Kenley has approached Premenstrual Syndrome in a spiritual way that can affect and help many women. Her story is not unlike many women who suffer. However, the manner in which she was able to combine her spirituality in helping her through life and dealing with PMS is tremendous. To be truly well, a woman needs to be balanced at home, at work, and spiritually.

The bottom line is that Premenstrual Syndrome does exist! It is treatable, and it can be controlled. I feel books such as Holli Kenley's can only help spread the word on how to control PMS and maintain personal balance.

To Wellness,
Marcia Fry-Galbraith
Director/Cofounder of the PMS
Center of California

Piece One

# Put Your Fears to Rest

# Questions About PMS?

Hopefully, you have picked up this book because you have some questions about PMS. You might be thinking to yourself, "What is PMS? Does it really exist? When does it happen? Do all women have PMS? Might I be one of them? Even if I thought I might have PMS, where could I go for help, and more importantly, why would anyone want to help me? Isn't PMS something that women are just supposed to live with and stop complaining about it?"

If you have thought about any of the above questions, you are not alone. Thousands of women think these thoughts everyday, and unfortunately, many of them do not ever pursue the answers. I believe that is not because they do not want the answers—it is because they are fearful of the responses they may confront by simply asking the questions.

You see, for over twenty years of my life I was fearful to ask questions about my health. Because I had never heard of PMS, my only answer for myself was that I was indeed crazy. Therefore, I suffered severely and needlessly. This scenario absolutely need not be the case for women today. PMS is being diagnosed and treated successfully all over the world. Women are becoming educated about PMS, taking responsibility for their health, reestablishing new and better relationships, and reaching out to support others. If you think you, or someone you know, might suffer from PMS (or even if you are not sure what PMS is), this book will be the beginning of a new journey for you. It will provide you with answers to some fundamental questions about PMS supported through the latest research of the most respected experts in the field. In it I will share my own battle with PMS and my quest for recovery. Let me put your fears to rest and bring you the hope and comfort I received. And, I will show you the solutions (road maps) God has uncovered to guide us through our journey successfully toward peace.

# What Is Premenstrual Syndrome?

PMS is physical disorder in which there is an imbalance of progesterone in relation to the amount of estrogen present in a woman's body premenstrually. This hormonal imbalance manifests itself in both physical as well as psychological symptoms. The physical symptoms are the ones that most women feel free to talk about—the headaches, backaches, bloatedness, fatigue, breast tenderness, and increased hunger. The psychological symptoms are the ones that women tend to avoid admitting—let alone to share or discuss them with a friend. They include feelings of depression, tension, anxiety, irritability, forgetfulness, abusiveness, crying, confusion, frustration, mood swings, uncontrollable rages, guilt feelings, and thoughts of suicide.

One of the most important facts to note about PMS is that if a woman does indeed suffer from the illness, she does NOT suffer from these symptoms all month long. The only way to accurately diagnose PMS (according to British PMS specialist, Dr. Katharina Dalton) is to chart the symptoms on a menstrual chart. The symptoms must be present every month for at least a period of three months, symptoms must be present premenstrually and cannot start before the onset of ovulation, and there must be a complete absence of symptoms for at least seven days (Dalton 17). One other crucial aspect in diagnosing PMS is that the symptoms are of sufficient severity to interfere with some aspect of living (Bender 6). Only by charting can a woman and her doctor identify whether or not she suffers from a pattern of symptoms. It is also important to note that there is not one set pattern of symptoms that lead to diagnosis of PMS. A woman may find herself fitting into one of these common patterns:

1. Symptoms may occur from just one day and up to ten days prior to menstruation and continue until the onset of menstruation.

2. Symptoms may occur at ovulation, resolve in a day or two, and then reappear later on in the premenstrual phase.

**3.** Symptoms may occur at ovulation, and continue on until the onset of menstruation.

**4.** Symptoms may occur at ovulation, continue on steadily through the menstrual period, and resolving toward the end of the menstrual period (Norris 12).

> No matter what pattern a woman can identify with, if she does NOT experience a symptom-free phase lasting at least seven days following the pattern, PMS cannot be the correct diagnosis for her.

From the patterns above, one can see that PMS symptoms can last anywhere from one day and even as much as 15-20 days. Just as there is great fluctuation in the duration of the symptoms, there is also a wide range in the degrees of severity of the symptoms. For example, a woman could suffer from mild symptoms (slight weight gain, moodiness, fatigue) for just a day or two, while another woman might suffer from severe symptoms (deep depression, hysteria, food cravings) for a week or two. The important point is that if indeed a woman is suffering from PMS—whether is be mild, moderate, or even severe—there is help available.

In diagnosing PMS it is extremely important to be aware of the fact that the onset of PMS can occur at different times in one's life. In other words, a woman could be completely symptom-free for a long period of time. And then, she may begin to experience PMS because she has begun taking the birth control pill, or she has discontinued use of the pill. One of my sisters was symptom-free until she had a tubal ligation. Then, she began to experience marked irritability, anxiety, and crying episodes to the point that it disrupted her personal life. Certain landmarks can aid a woman and her physician in the diagnosis of PMS, such as—PMS can begin at puberty, after pregnancy, or after an episode of amenorrhea (no periods) (Norris 10).

As a woman and her physician are reviewing her history, Dr.

Ronald Norris suggests they look out for the following:

 **Times of increased severity**

Perhaps a woman has had mild PMS symptoms for a number of years, but then she notes a marked increase in the severity of the symptoms due to discontinued use of the pill, or after cessation of breast-feeding, or after a tubal ligation or a hysterectomy.

 **Painless menstruation**

Painful menstruation is not part of the PMS diagnosis. However, pain or pelvic discomfort before menstruation may be a part of PMS.

 **Weight fluxuations**

Many women suffering from PMS experience weight swings from 6-9 pounds.

 **Food cravings**

Many women experience food cravings, increased appetite, and eating binges during their premenstruum. They especially crave sweet and salty foods. Also, women suffering from PMS experience acute symptoms, severe headaches, violent outbursts when they go four to five hours without food intake.

 **Intolerance for alcohol**

Women with PMS may find that they have a decreased tolerance to alcohol during their premenstruum. And, yet, they may find that they crave alcohol.

**Inability to tolerate the birth control pill**

Women with PMS find that they do not tolerate the birth control pill well. They experience weight gain, headaches, depression, and exacerbation of the PMS symptoms they already have.

 **History of postpartum depression**

Many women with PMS have been found to have suffered from postpartum depression (to the extent of which they were hospitalized or received some kind of psychiatric treatment).

 **History of threatened miscarriage**

Women who have had bleeding in the first months of pregnancy followed by a successful pregnancy is common in PMS cases.

 **History of toxemia**

Toxemia (significant fluid retention) or hypertension during pregnancy.

 **Increased sex drive**

Women suffering from PMS may experience an increase in sex drive during the premenstruum. However, if the woman is also experiencing depression, she may in fact experience a decrease in sex drive. (Norris 11-12)

As you can see, PMS has been successfully diagnosed following proven guidelines. Doctors and clinicians know what PMS is, they know when it is most likely to occur, and they know how it will occur (in what patterns it takes it's form). The question is "Do you know if you might have PMS?" I didn't know for a long time what was wrong with me, but I do remember thinking this one thought hundreds of times, *I just don't feel like myself.* I could not pin-point it, but I knew I wasn't ME. Have you ever had this thought, even if it was just for a day or two? As you read my story, see if you (or perhaps someone you know) can identify with the feelings, emotions, or situations that I encountered. Part of becoming well with PMS is the wonderful peace of mind that comes with knowing that you are not alone in your suffering. Let me share mine with you now.

Piece Two

# Accepting My Own PMS

# What's Wrong With Me?

"Why do I feel so good today? Why do I sometimes feel great for several days or even a week or two, and then I feel like a different person?"

A little voice in my head says, "You are unstable...you are not like other women...you are a failure."

I shake my head to make the little voice go away. More questions flood my mind. "Why do I lose control over my behavior for no apparent reason and fly into violent fits of rage, anger, and hysteria?"

The voice returns, only louder this time, "You are worthless, you can't even control your own actions. You are losing it!"

I tell myself it is not true. I tell the voice to go away. Immediately, another question pops in my mind, "How much more of the depression can I take? I already feel such regret, shame, and embarrassment for my irrational behaviors... must I feel even more?"

A resounding voice says, "Yes, you are a nothing. No one loves you—how could they—after what you said and did? You would be better off dead."

My mind quickly argues back with the stinging voice, "But that can't be true, it can't be true. There must be someone I can turn to...someone who can help me with my secret pain...there must be an answer or a reason for all of this?"

"THERE IS," the piercing voice returns. "YOU ARE CRAZY!"

I shout back, "I won't let that voice get to me. Where is He?" I cry out, "God, are you there? Can You help me?" There is a tugging inside of me, mostly at my heart, but I can't tell who it is or what's happening. My pleas continue, "Oh, God, why don't you hear me, why don't you answer me?"

Questions begin to fill my mind again. "How long must I struggle with this bizarre and debilitating battle for my physical well-being as well as for my sanity? Should I give up or even end my life?"

The destructive voice explodes in my head, "YES, GIVE UP. YOU ARE OF NO USE TO ANYONE!"

I grab my head, trying to keep my thoughts in focus, wishing and hoping for answers. Far off in the distance, but closer than I know or even realize, an extremely faint but gentle voice whispers, "Hold on Holli, Trust me...I'm with you all the way."

# Confusion

My senior year is just about over! I should be excited; I guess I am today. There is so much to look forward to—the Graduating Class of 1969, the Senior ALL-NIGHT-Party, the Senior Ball, and most of all—starting college! It seems as though I just can't wait to leave this hum-drum town of Stockton. There has got to be more to life than this! Anyway, I should be proud of myself. I've worked hard these past four years and I've got the grades to show it. In a class of almost 900, I'm graduating twelfth—a 3.86 isn't bad. Also, I made it as a life-time member of CSF (California Scholarship Federation) which is a really big honor in the State of California. I've been accepted to the University of California at Santa Barbara—it wasn't my first choice, but it's beautiful there—the ocean and the surfers can be seen just outside my dorm window!

As I come home from school, I do my usual things: have a snack, do my homework, practice my flute, do more homework, and help out with dinner. When I have a moment, I sit down to jot something down in my diary or at least to look through it. I have an odd feeling as I read through the pages. As my eyes scan the words, it feels as though another person has written it—not me. I come across a page that describes a bad day. Nothing terrible has happened at school or at home—it is just one of those" days. My words seem dark and heavy—sadness and depression are evident. I think back and I remember that day, or several days, as I flip through the diary...

...I recall turning out the lights in my bedroom on of those nights. I feel dark inside—and alone, very alone. I lay down on the floor of my bedroom and begin to sob—not cry (crying is too gentle a word). I feel as though I am in a pit, and I can't climb out. And, worst of all, no one cares if I live or die. Self-pity overcomes me as I curl into a fetal position and rock myself to sleep. It will be okay in the morning—it will go away—at least for awhile.

When morning comes, I have responsibilities—school, French Club, Youth Symphony, and of course, homework and practicing. Put on that smile and get going—whatever happens, I don't want to be late. I HATE being late! Motor through the day—do your best—remember that every day counts and school isn't over yet. When I get home, I can go into my room and lie down—and feel what I feel (but not at school—never there).

As I arrive home, I quickly go through my routine. I feel weary—pretending to be cheerful all day is very tiring. The slightest let-down seems overwhelming. I take out my flute to practice—those long tone scales just aren't coming together. I become easily frustrated and angry. Tension fills by body and mind. I pick up my precious instrument (one that I have devoted six years to) and throw it across the room. Tears burn in my eyes. I might have damaged one of the few things that I value so much. But, what does it matter? Nothing matters; I don't, that's for sure. I throw myself on the bed holding my head tightly. Sometimes, it feels like it might explode. I cry out something that really makes no sense to me: "God, dear God, help me."

The next morning, I wake up wondering if this day will be like the last. I don't feel rested, but then I do not seem to sleep all that well lately. Today is Friday, so things can't be all that bad! I've got to get through my day—an important test in history, and English composition due, and the last chance to practice for that concert coming up in advanced band. Also, I have a date tonight with Bill—can't afford to be moody!

Again, I feel fatigued as I walk through the door into my house at the end of the day. My head feels heavy—confusion seems to blur my usual clear and precise thoughts. I don't really feel like going out tonight, but I miss Bill and I want to see him. Besides, if I don't straighten up and show him that I can be fun to be with, he might break up with me.

As I'm getting ready, I look closely in the mirror. Why is it that I don't feel pretty? I fuss with my hair and make-up, do and redo, do and redo. I am not satisfied. I become angry and tension-filled. I pull at my hair and throw my brush. I feel like screaming or yelling. Instead, I cry hard, then harder. I curl up on the bathroom floor asking myself a question that I've asked so many times before, "What is wrong with me? Please, someone, what is wrong with me?"

I cancel my date with Bill. Instead of being with him, I pull myself together enough to wash my face, get ready for bed, and get out my diary. Sometimes if I write in the diary or work on some poetry, it's helpful or therapeutic. Getting those feelings out on paper somehow brings a focus to the hysteria. Or, at least it does for the moment anyway. Later, those same words seem so far away—so distant from the person reading them only a few days or a week or so later.

As I close my diary, I spend a few moments reflecting upon my words and my life. Although I had written that diary entry just a couple of days ago, I feel so good today (I had started my menstrual cycle but, of course, I had no reason to connect how I felt with my period). How could I write something so sad, so desperate? There is so much to look forward to, like tonight, is the Senior Awards Dinner. I've got to get ready. Whatever happens I don't want to be late!

*******

Wow! The unbelievable has happened! I can't wait to tell my parents. I run into the house and share with them that their daughter was named Outstanding Senior Girl in the Graduating Class of 1969! They actually chose me when there were so many other qualified girls. There is nothing that can get me down—nothing!

Getting ready for bed that night, I again pick up my diary. I write something very positive—it will help to balance out the negative. I make a promise to myself that those down times" won't bother me again. I won't LET them!

For the first time in several nights, I fall into a deep sleep—my eyes feel heavy and my head light. The weight of the world seems to lift from my body. I feel a slight sensation of peacefulness—I secretly wish that it would last a lifetime.

Little do I know that those dark times will return—more strongly and severely than ever before.

# Secrets

As I sit here among the many college graduates, I can't believe it's finally here! Four long years of studying, practicing, finals, papers, mid-terms, recitals, practice rooms and lectures are finished. That last quarter of twenty-one units and the TA (Teacher's Assistant) for the professor, plus working a part time clerical job in Santa Barbara, in addition to doing my everyday things just about did me in—but I made it! It feels great to have accomplished the goals that I set for myself—even if I had to adjust them just a little. I've got my major in French and a minor in music (I wished it were the other way around), and I've experienced an incredible college life living away from home these past four years.

As I look upon the stage, the first speaker begins to address the crowd. My mind reflects back to that first year when I naively and excitedly entered into the mainstream of college life. I lived in a girl's (only) dormitory way up on the eighth floor. The view was beautiful from the small window with the sprawling modern Spanish buildings nestled among a mixture of old and odd architectural wonders named after their respective donors. And, off to the right was an almost perfectly line grove of eucalyptus trees, standing at attention, and birds of varying species flying freely from them calling as though they were waiting for an answer. Off to the left was my favorite sight - the mysterious lagoon. It was surrounded by drooping trees, thickly woven bushes, and a myriad of animals—each making its home in the secretive passage ways and shelters that the lagoon provided. As I stood at the window, I could often times hear the sound of the ocean— ever so slightly, but just enough to bring a peacefulness over me. I cherished those moments of tranquility and beauty because oftentimes they were interrupted with days of deep pain, and sorrow, and regret.

One such memory clearly stands out in my mind. It took place during the later part of the first quarter of school. I was keeping myself extremely busy - taking a full load of classes (mostly music), spending a horrendous number of hours in the practice rooms, playing in a campus musical (which required numerous practices as well as performances), taking care of my personal needs and also maintaining a fun and exciting relationship with a guy I had met since coming to college. My mid-terms had gone well, and I really felt that I was on top of things. In other words, I felt good - in fact- really good about my first stab at being a college girl.

Then, one night after a performance of the musical, I was walking back to my dorm alone. Several friends had offered to walk with me, but I declined. I just didn't feel like talking to anyone. I had been on edge for a few days, and I didn't want to have to watch my every word. I stopped by my boyfriend's dorm along the way only to find him visiting with another girl. Normally, this wouldn't have bothered me, but this night was different.

We exchanged an unpleasant set of words which then led to a shouting match (something we were totally unaccustomed to). My anger took hold of me like it had never done before. I felt so out of control. Before I embarrassed myself further, I ran out of the room and down the hallway.

Racing to the elevator, I frantically waited for the doors to open. My mind was rushing, my head was spinning, and my heart was pounding so hard it hurt my chest. Once in the elevator, I tried to catch my breath, but I felt out of control. I was frightened by my own emotions. "What is happening to me?" I thought. "Why did I 'flip out' like that? How could I act that way?"

When the doors opened, my first thought was to get to my room where I could feel safe and where I could calm myself. But, when I opened to the door and sat down on my bed, I felt even more out of control—this time though was even worse. That pit that I would often feel myself falling into was now pulling me down. I felt myself sinking faster and faster. I needed to talk to someone - quickly. My roommate was gone, so I checked across the hallway for my best friend. She was not there either.

Strange thoughts started invading my mind: "No one cares...if they did, they would be here...where did they go...I don't have anyone who can help me..." Slowly, I walked over to my dresser where I kept my cosmetics. I opened the top cabinet and I looked into the mirror. I told myself, "You are a nothing. You'd be better off dead." Carefully, I removed the razor blade from my razor and held it against my wrist. I turned my head to the right and cut as quickly as possible. I staggered over to my bed, curled up in a ball and...

*******

When I woke up in the hospital, there was one thought that kept running through my mind, "What would my friends and family think and say?" It seemed so odd that was so important to me; but, it was! I was a good girl, a hard working girl, a people-pleaser. "What would they think of me now?"

After a couple of days of observation and an agreement to see a psychiatrist twice a week for at least ten weeks, I was released from the hospital. My parents were reluctant to let me stay at school, but I convinced them that it was better for me to finish my classes and to feel good about completing the quarter.

By the following week, things were back to normal (and I had started my menstrual period; however, I had no idea that it possibly could relate to my feeling better). I remember standing outside one of my classrooms waiting for my turn in taking my piano final. How odd this all is, I thought. A few days ago I wanted to end my life. Now, I just want to go in that room and play the best Beethoven Sonata that I am capable of performing. My name was called and I walked in and sat down at the piano. I looked down at my hands and saw my bandaged wrist. I looked over at my piano teacher—he smiled and told me to begin. "Life can be so lovely—so good," I thought. "Why would I ever want to hurt myself?'

Oh my gosh! They are calling the names of the graduates. As the announcer calls out the names beginning with "C," my best friend comes to mind.

We roomed together in an apartment during our sophomore year, and we traveled to France together our junior year on an education abroad program. Carol was a wonderful friend, more like a sister, and her parents were like my second family to me. As I think back on those two years, there were so many fantastic memories – like the time Carol and I traveled to London with two other girls for a two week vacation. Can you imagine what four twenty-year-old girls found to do in a city like London!? I remember when Carol and I became little sisters to one of the fraternities and one of our first assignments was to sneak in and steal all of the guys' underwear from their rooms! And, I recall our cooking–we thought it was so great. Little did we know that hardly anyone else could stand it! Carol was a stabilizing force for me – she boosted me up when I was down. But, during those two years, I also learned something very valuable (or at least I thought it was at the time) – how to hide my periods of depression. I didn't ever want anyone to feel sorry for me or to worry that I might try to hurt myself again, so I made a promise to myself that no one would know about my secret – including Carol.

There are places where one can learn to let go of her horrible feelings without anyone else knowing–the shower is the best place. With the water rushing down, the fan blowing noisily, and the door closed tightly, the tears that I have held for so long would come gushing out ever so freely. The sobs that would shake my body were hidden behind the curtain and my clenching fists would find a release in the squeezing of a wet cloth. Privacy provides an escape for confused emotions, and reddened eyes can be blamed on soap and shampoo.

Another hiding place is in my bed at night. Here, the cry of pain must be kept more quiet, but it's a place of comfort. Again, the tears are free to flow. The pillow serves a dual purpose – as a receptacle for the salty water and as a buffer for muted cries of anguish that accidentally slip out. And, in my room I can turn on the radio–music always comforts and relaxes me.

Good heavens, the H's are being called. I'd better stand up and act like I know what is going on! Wow, this is great. It is almost my turn. Here goes...."Holli Rae Hull." Oh, I wish my parents were here! They would be so proud. I return to my seat with my diploma and breathe a sigh of relief. This fourth and last year was a struggle. I had pushed myself really hard, but there was no excuse for those dark times to have gotten the better of me. I think about the time that I received a C on my report card. Normally, yes, I would be disappointed, but I wouldn't have reacted the way that I did in this case.

As I was cleaning up my apartment, the mail arrived. I was tired and had not been feeling myself for a few days. I had really wanted to get all A's and B's, and I was sure that I would. When I opened up my report card, I just couldn't believe my eyes! I had received a C in one of my classes. My mind just went crazy. I started swearing, yelling, throwing things, and running around the apartment like a mad person. Suddenly, I felt as though the room were caving in on me - the walls were coming closer and closer together! I ran for the door and flew out of the room I ran and ran and ran. I was crying hysterically and could hardly catch my breath. Soon, I was out in a field, and I found myself standing in the middle of a swarm of bees! Normally, this would frighten me silly, because I am deathly allergic to bees. However, I just stood there—in fact—I lay down and began laughing like a maniac. When the laughter subsided, it turned to tears, then sobs, then extreme fatigue. I pulled myself up and carefully maneuvered my way out of the swarm of bees. As I found my way home, I remember looking up into the sky and asking that same question one more time, "Why God? Why me?"

It's over! Everybody is cheering, laughing, hugging, and throwing their caps. What a great day! And there is so much to look forward to—I'll be going on to Sacramento State University to work on my teaching credential. It will be a lot of work, but I'm ready. I'm stronger now—I've made it through four difficult years—certainly one to two more will be a breeze. And most importantly, my secret is under control—or should I say well hidden. Even better, no one will know me there—or will know of my past. It will be a fresh start...at least, I hope it will be.

# Desperation

Wow! I can't believe I'm here—Hawaii! Standing on my balcony of this lovely hotel room overlooking the blue-green waters of Oahu, I feel a peace and a joy that runs through my soul. I've really earned this vacation—it's my reward to myself for completing my teaching credential. It has certainly been worth two years of hard work. Now, I can get a teaching job and be self sufficient. But, for the next two weeks, I'm going to completely relax—lie on the warm soft sand, run my face and body through the clean fresh waters, and tan my skin in the rays of the sun.

As I look out into the waves and hear them crashing against the shore, I feel so thankful for being here—and being alive. However, life continues to puzzle me. Its beauty and its ugliness seem to manifest themselves in me in such complex and extreme degrees. I wonder why my life doesn't have a balance and a consistency to it. I don't understand why I still struggle with periodic days of deep depression, and yet there are weeks where I feel on top of the world. Every time I have a relapse, I promise myself that it won't happen again, but it always does.

I lie back in a lounge chair watching the tourists and the islanders, but most of all, I stare into the ocean. The rushing of the water brings forth a memory that I've tried to suppress time and time again.

My schedule had been a nightmare—student teaching in the morning from 8:00 A.M. to 12:00 P.M., then over to Cal State for more education classes until about 3:00 P.M., then off to my job at a department store until at least 8:00 P.M., then finally home for a quick dinner before homework, and hopefully, some sleep. I thought I should be able to handle this schedule. I was always an extremely organized person, and I always managed to get everything done and done well. However, I had been feeling somewhat stressed over the past couple of days—just not quite myself. This night, I had an additional worry—it was my boyfriend's birthday. I had made a cake the night before and wrapped his presents so that everything would be ready when I got home. I wanted everything to be perfect.

I arrived home in plenty of time. I put the cake out on the kitchen table with the birthday presents neatly arranged around it. I even placed the candles on the cake with the matches set to the side so that I could light them as soon as I heard the car pull up. It was just about 9:00 P.M., and I knew my boyfriend should show up at any moment. I sat down in the living room and waited. One hour went by, then two, then three. All this time, the anxiety within me built and built. It was not like anger - it was a tension that felt as though my head were going to explode. I was pacing the room like a tiger pacing in its cage. I tried to calm myself but I couldn't. Finally, I heard a car door shut. As my boyfriend came to the door, I opened it—only to find him drunk. He stumbled into the house falling over the furniture.

For a moment, I just held my breath. Then, the explosion came. I began yelling and screaming at him. I grabbed for the presents and began hurling them at him. The cards and gifts were flying around the room and all he could do was laugh. The anger then totally took hold of me; I had no control over myself whatsoever—nor did I want to. At that point, I didn't care what happened.

Suddenly, I rushed towards him. With my arms and fists, I began pounding on his head, back and shoulders as hard as I could. At that moment, I could not stop myself. I was crying hysterically, still yelling and gasping for air. Every bit of energy was being drained from my body. My hands began to ache and I felt a sharp pain on my right hand. I looked down and saw blood dripping from my fingers - my rings had cut and torn my own flesh. My boyfriend was on his knees with his arms over his head. I stopped suddenly, as though someone had hit me. I cried out, "Oh my God, what have I done?"

Slowly, my boyfriend got up and left. I stood at the kitchen sink with the cold water running over the cuts on my fingers. My hands were stinging but nothing came close to the burn of desperation inside my body. I began to cry, then sob. My body jerked with the cries of regret and anguish. That question once again entered my mind, "Why God? Why is this happening to me?"

A few weeks later an incident happened that, at the time, I did not understand or appreciate, but which nevertheless was very important. In order to earn some extra money, I had taken a job selling cosmetics at in-home parties. The woman who was helping me to get started had invited me over to her home to get some supplies, go over the selling routine, and to plan out my schedule. Once we were done with our business, we somehow started talking about God. Since I knew nothing about God, I didn't say much. Shortly after, she pulled out a little booklet and she asked me if I would like to accept the Lord into my life. Since I really didn't know what that meant, and I didn't think it would hurt me, I said yes.

She read the booklet and asked me the questions at the bottom of each page. I answered yes to each question without really understanding what was being asked. When we completed the last page, she closed the booklet and she gave me a big hug. There were tears in her eyes. I was totally confused as to why, but she was a nice person and so I hugged her back.

I didn't sell the cosmetics for very long of a time. I was terrible at getting people to buy things, and I also just didn't have enough time. So, I never saw or heard from this woman friend again. However, the booklet, the questions, and the yes responses that I had given, remained clearly in my mind for a long time.

Goodness! I'm wasting valuable tanning time sitting here up on my balcony. I'm going to put on my swimsuit and go for a walk along the beach.

Quickly, I change my clothes, take the elevator down from the fifteenth floor and walk through the hotel lobby amazed at the natural beauty of the flora. The breeze gently blows through my hair and the smell of the ocean entices me to hurry on to the beach. I drop my towel and lotions in the sand and begin my stroll down the shore. I let my feet and ankles get caught in the teasing tide, and I laugh to myself as I see my funny footprints in the sand. The ocean has always been a source of peace for me. Often times I wish I could bottle it up and take it with me.

As I look into the rushing white foam, I think of the time when the cold feel of water temporarily saved my sanity.

I had come home from my usual day of teaching, school, and work, and I felt extremely tired. In fact, I was utterly exhausted. I had not felt like myself for a few days but I was sure it would pass. I was worried about getting a teaching job in the fall. Jobs were far and few between, and there were a dozen teachers available for each position listed. I had been sending out applications weekly, even to places I had no intentions of living. But, I had hoped to receive a positive response from somewhere. Just obtaining an interview would help!

I looked over at the mail on the floor by the front door. I hesitated for a moment before I picked it up, but thought there just might be a chance for something positive. Each piece of mail that wasn't a bill read similarly: We are sorry to inform you that we are not hiring at this point in time. If we anticipate any job openings, we will contact you for an interview at that time. Thank you for your interest in our school district.

On a good day, this would not have bothered me too much. But today was different. I felt such rejection. I began to blame my lack of a teaching position on my inadequacies. My mind began to run through the set of tapes that frequently accompany these dark sessions. Over and over I kept hearing a voice (like an enemy inside my mind) saying, "You are worthless. No one will ever hire you. You can't even control your own mind." I held my head in my hands telling myself, "Don't let this happen... get control... hold on..." But, I felt myself slipping into that pit of despair.

My head felt as though it were going to explode. I kept pressing it tighter and tighter with my hands but the pounding wouldn't stop. I started shaking, afraid of what I might do. I could never repeat what I had once attempted—although I wanted to. I could feel the wall next to me and suddenly I turned and started pounding my head against it as hard as I could. Pain shot through my eyes as the tears flowed down my burning cheeks. I knew this banging must stop, but how? For some reason, I ran to the bathroom and flung open the shower door. I blasted on the cold water and threw myself in—clothes and all.

For many moments—I can't say how long—I stood there. The cold rushing water soothed my aching head and cooled my hot face. My hands clutched the faucets, stabilizing my body as it jerked freely from hysterical crying. I lifted my face up into the running water and I cried out loudly, "Help me, God. Please help me."

As I work my toes through the seaweed, that darkness seems so far away from the light that fills my life today. As I look up into the beautiful sky, I think about how I cried out to God. I wonder, "Is He up there? Did He hear me when I cried out? If so, why didn't He answer?" I tell myself that perhaps there is no God, but I don't really want to believe that. For some reason, even though God was never discussed in my household growing up, I have always believed that He existed. I still want to believe it. My eyes spy an unusually shaped shell. As I reach for it, I think to myself, "Only God could make something so perfect and lovely."

Looking out into the silvery shining waters, I start speaking to God. I feel silly. A thought enters my mind, "God can't help me until I help myself. That's it! Once I can get myself under control, then He'll love me enough to help me along. I can do it! I'm stronger than I ever was before." I turn my back to the setting sun and walk away.

Unknowingly, I turn my back on the only source of real help that I will desperately need in the years to come.

# Pain And Shame

As I lie nestled in the warm moist soft blankets, tears of joy roll down the sides of my face. I stare up at the gray drab ceiling, but somehow even it looks lovely right now. I have just given birth to a six pound two ounce precious baby girl. Her name is Alexis Raechel. How very fortunate I am. I have so much to be thankful for. These past four years have been good to me - a great teaching job back in my hometown of Stockton, living near my family and friends, a wonderful husband, a beautiful home, and now a little girl! I doze off for a minute relaxing in my moment of tranquility.

Suddenly, I'm jolted by the soft voice but rough hands of the nurse. She has come in to massage my abdomen—making sure the blood does not clot but moves freely from my body (a procedure necessary after giving birth). No one has informed me of this very painful and irritating procedure. The nurse assures me that this will be over soon, but somehow it doesn't lessen the sharpness of the motions.

As she finishes, I take deep breaths, relieved that the pain subsides rather quickly. Oh, how I wish that I was capable of eliminating other kinds of pain with such speed. Even though the past four years have been filled with happiness and blessings, I still struggle with those days of darkness. I think of my husband and the things I have put him through.

It was two years ago, in the fall of 1977, when John (then my fiance´) and I had gone to a shopping mall out of town to look for a wedding dress. We had spent a couple of hours looking in several shops but there was nothing that really seemed to please me. In fact, with each passing boutique, I found myself becoming extremely irritated by the frustration of shopping, pushy people, crowds, and even John! He had stopped at one little store to look at some sun glasses. I rudely questioned him about his selfishness in shopping for sun glasses when I needed to find a wedding dress! I had said it loudly enough that I embarrassed him in front of several people; but frankly, I didn't really care.

John gently took me by the arm and escorted me out of the store. He asked me what the problem was. This was my opportunity to blow. And did I. Without raising my voice too loudly, I proceeded to tear him to pieces verbally, using crude and vulgar language. My tongue was out of control and the more I spoke, the more the rage began to build. John attempted to calm me, but all that did was infuriate me further. Suddenly, I grabbed my car keys from my purse and told him to find his own way home; I was leaving. As I turned and ran out of the mall, John followed behind. I found myself out in the parking lot, dashing around like a mad person. I started crying, feeling confused and ashamed. People were looking at me wondering what I was doing. Finally, I spotted the car. While I was rushing over to it, John caught up with me. He tried desperately to reason with me but I was humiliated, angry, and embarrassed. I pushed him out of the way, unlocked the car, got in, and recklessly drove away (almost hitting John in the process). I didn't drive far—mostly because I couldn't see from crying so hard. I pulled over and allowed my body and mind to release the surge of emotions. Through the sobs, I kept thinking, "How could I treat John this way? He is so good to me. Why can't I control this? What will he do?"

After I composed myself, I started the car and drove around looking for John. I found him standing on the sidewalk in front of the mall, waiting for the cab he had called. I got out of the car, and apologized. Together, we got back in the car and drove home. The incident was never discussed. I was quiet and withdrawn for a few days, sorting out my shame and regret. John was cautious and loving. I don't think he knew what to do any more than I did.

Ouch! The nurse is back—time for the massage again. She informs me that this must be done every twenty minutes for the next couple of hours. Why don't they tell you about these things in Lamaze? I ask, "When I can see and hold my little girl?" She says, "As soon as you're out of recovery".

John comes into the room to see how I'm doing. He smiles as he approaches the bed and he takes my hand. He tells me she is beautiful. I smile and the tears of contentment flow freely. Because he is so accustomed to tears of sadness, he asks me if everything is alright. I reassure him that I'm fine, but as I look into his eyes, I see that frightened, helpless expression that I bring forth in him often.

I close my eyes for a moment and think about the sadness. Right now, at this very moment, it seems so foreign to me. But, without failure, in a few days, or perhaps a few weeks, it will be there. It always starts with FRUSTRATION, ANGER, and or TENSION, followed by intensified ANXIETY and RESTLESSNESS, and then deep DEPRESSION. I've tried to shut myself off from John when the first two stages occur, and by the time the depression sets in, I am basically harmless. I curl up in bed and cry, and cry, and cry. I don't know what to do for myself and neither does John. He just looks at me with deep concern and worry. I, on the other hand, keep questioning God, and myself, and more and more often, I begin to doubt my sanity.

Finally, the nurse brings our little one to us. I sit up just enough to hold her comfortably in my arms. John and I stroke her head, face, and hands as we marvel at her. It is such a special moment—one that I will always remember. I think to myself, "God is amazing. Only He can put together this little person. He is good." I close my eyes and start to speak to Him, but then, decide to just promise myself something: "I will be a good mother. I won't feel down ever again (especially now that I have a baby to take care of). I'll be extra strong now that I have to be."

The nurse gently lifts the baby from my arms and asks is there is anything I need. I answer quietly, "No," but there is a strange tugging at my heart that tells me, "Yes."

# Darkness

I pull my car in the closest parking space to the condominium where I'll be staying. As I open the car door, the smell of the ocean, the cry of the sea gulls, and the rustle of the reeds immediately calm my spirit. It's good to be here—my special place of peace.

I've always loved Pajaro Dunes. Its privacy, quietness, solitude, and beauty are hard-pressed to find elsewhere. I've enjoyed coming here with family and friends, but mostly I escape here in time of need. This time I've come alone on purpose. Alexis is with her grandparents. John is in Stockton. I've come here this time looking for some answers to some very difficult questions. Only this time, I know who to ask.

After I get unpacked and settled, I take a walk along the beach. It's breezy and cold, but the brisk air feels good against my face. I've bundled up in a turtleneck, sweatshirt, and jeans, but I leave my feet bare to feel the sand squish between my toes. There is no one around. I can have some quiet time with God. Yes, He is now a part of my life. Actually, He always was; I just didn't know it. As I watch the waves crashing and water spraying, I think of when we met and when I asked Him into my life–this time for real.

Alexis was getting ready to turn two, and I was looking for a pre-school for her. After asking around, I was given several good recommendations for a Christian-based program located next to a church just two blocks from our home. I called and asked for an appointment to visit the school and meet the administrators.

The following week, I spent an entire morning observing the classrooms, looking over the curriculum, and talking with the people in charge. I was extremely impressed with their program and most pleased with the warmth and love that I felt in each of the classrooms. I enrolled Alexis for the fall term.

Each day, when I picked up Alexis from pre-school, I was always treated with genuine kindness from the staff. I got to know the head administrators quite well. They were an older couple who immediately felt like second parents to me. One day, as we were talking, they asked me if I would like to come to church some Sunday. I said I would talk to John about it. It sounded like a fine idea to me.

John was hesitant at first, but within a few weeks we had decided to try it. We both were overwhelmed by the love and acceptance we were shown. No one was pushy or overbearing. The members simply made us feel wanted and special. Both John and I were amazed at the sermons. It seemed as though each one was directed specifically to us. Our questions were answered, our hearts were filled, and our souls were uplifted. Each Sunday we left, looking forward to the next.

A few months after attending, John and I accepted the Lord into our lives. Although it was an extremely moving moment, it seemed like a very natural thing to do. As we went forward to the alter, that tugging at my heart I had felt for two years stopped. I knew now who was trying to get my attention.

A short time after the altar call, John and I were baptized together. This, too, was a time I will never forget. Giving my testimony, I realized for the first time how much I needed God in my life. For so long, I had tried to make it on my own, and I had failed. As the pastor submerged me into the water, I felt a cleansing and chance for a new beginning.

As a new Christian, there were so many things that I didn't know. However, I quickly became involved in a Bible study and active in church activities. I wanted to educate myself as much as possible. I believed (or wanted to believe) that because I was now a Christian, my problems would go away or that God would automatically protect me from any harm. I want to stress that no one taught me this, it was just something I thought.

This, however, was far from the truth. Although I loved the Lord and I continued to grow in my Christian walk, I was still plagued with those days of darkness. In fact, in some respects, it got mush worse.

There were days when my emotions felt like a roller-coaster—constantly up and down, up and down. At times, I was so filled with tension and anxiety that my hands shook as I tried to put on my make-up or drink my coffee. And, even my teaching had been affected. Several times, I had called in sick or left school early in order to come home to let out the depression that had filed my stomach to the point where I felt I would vomit.

Sometimes, I would get angry at God. I didn't understand why He wouldn't help me—especially now—when He was a part of my life.

A big wave comes crashing down and the water rushes up to my pant legs. Burrrr...that's cold! It's getting dark and I head back towards the condominium. Before I walk away, I give thanks to God for this beauty, for His wonder, and His majesty. I also pray that He will help me with the problem I now face—one much greater than I've ever had before.

Sitting by the fire, listening to soft music in one ear and the sound of the waves pounding in the other, I eat my dinner. The warmth of the fire relaxes me—and I can feel the tension and anxiety from the days before leave my body. I lay my head back on the couch and think about what has happened—about where I went wrong.

John and I filed for divorce after nearly six years of marriage. I can't believe it is really happening—I thought we would be together forever. I've sorted through my life, again and again, and I believe that I must hold myself responsible for many of the failures.

Although there are other problems, I know in my heart that the difficult times that I systematically go through have not only taken their toll on me, but on John and Alexis as well. I realize that I am an extremely complex and challenging person to live with. With each episode of darkness, I experience extreme guilt and regret. In turn, that remorse chisels away at my self-worth, self-esteem, and self-respect. Because I feel so poorly about myself, I then turn to

John to fill that gap. My expectations for him are unrealistic, and when they are not met, I feel disappointed, unloved, and resentful. John, in turn, tries harder, becomes more frustrated, and then gives up because nothing he does can satisfy me anyway. John, too, then feels empty and unloved. The vicious cycle is frequently interrupted with days (often weeks) of normalcy; however, there are not enough consistent good days to allow for healing and communication to take place.

Gazing down at the glowing fire, I think about the talks that I have had with the Christian counselor whom I've been seeing for many months. Although he is very easy to talk to and I have been able to share my feelings and thoughts with him freely, there has been one thing that I have never mentioned (at least not directly): those recurring incidents of extreme rage, depression, and guilt. I have kept them somewhat secretive, believing them to be caused by a personality defect which causes me to be an insecure person. I told my counselor that "...this is just me—it's the way I am." I haven't wanted to share with him the ugly details of the reasons behind my inadequacies. I don't really know why except that I am ashamed and embarrassed. Also, I guess, I didn't think that he would understand. Truthfully, I believed he might think that I am crazy. Fearfully, there are times that I believe it myself.

Looking down at my watch, I see it is getting late. I clean up the dishes and get ready for bed. The fog has come in blocking the view of the white foam against the black waters but the sound of the waves pounding the ocean can still be heard easily from my bedroom. I climb into bed and while staring up into the dark, I prepare to speak to God, sensing something is not quite right. I get up, lie face down on the floor, arms straight out on both sides. With my eyes closed and my spirit humbled, I begin asking for God's forgiveness in my life. I talk about the divorce and all the pain and hurt it has brought to so many people. I talk about my failures as a wife, a mother, and a Christian. And lastly, I talk to him about the darkness in my life. Not only do I ask for his forgiveness, but I pray for His healing hand upon my mind, my body, and my spirit.

For some reason, this part of the prayer seems so

difficult. "Am I even ashamed to tell God of this problem?" Tears begin to flow unceasingly—not so much out of pain this time—but more out of a true releasing. I ask Him to help me, something I've asked Him before. However, this time, I feel myself letting go just a little.

Finishing my prayer, I give thanks to His Majesty for all His grace and mercy. I thank Him for giving me the strength to endure the consequences of the sin of divorce. And I thank Him for the courage to face each day— especially for the days of darkness—and for the hope He has given me that someday the darkness will cease to rob me of the joy that I so desperately seek in my life.

Drifting into a restful sleep, I give one last faint thanks that God protects us from knowing our future. Selfishly, I am frightened that His healing may take longer than I am able to endure.

# Craziness

*Good morning Sweetheart,*
*It is going to be a bright and shiny day!! I hope you had a good night's rest and you are ready to meet today's challenges. Keep 'bearing up'. I love you very much! It's a good day to be alive."*

*Dan*

As I look down at this kind and thoughtful note that my husband has written to me on my breakfast napkin, I think about how fortunate I am to have met and married such an understanding, forgiving, and positive man. Although we have been married for just a few months, Dan knows well the two sides of me. He, too, remains as confused and bewildered as I am as to why and how I can be an energetic, productive, enthusiastic, and outgoing woman for days and sometimes weeks, but then suddenly turn into an irrational, enraged, depressed, and guilt-ridden individual.

Even though it is extremely painful, Dan and I are able to talk about my problem. That communication has been and will probably be the saving grace of our marriage. We also pray together, not specifically for my problem, but for the strength to get through the dark times and the ability to forgive one another after painful and damaging episodes. Lately, it seems as though the occurrences have become more difficult to pull myself out of. As volatile as the anger was before, it has now intensified. Not too long ago, two such incidents happened where I thought I had lost it completely.

It was a short time before Dan and I were married. I was home after school on a Friday afternoon. Usually, I tried to get most of my house cleaning done before the weekend so that I would have time to do other things on Saturday and Sunday. Therefore, as soon as I got home, I hurriedly cleaned the bathrooms, mopped the floors, dusted, and started to vacuum. Dan had promised me that he would try to be at my house by 5:00 P.M. to help me with the vacuuming.

I was extremely tired on this Friday, and I knew that trying to do all this housework was really not a good idea, but I proceeded anyway. By the time 5:00 P.M. rolled around, I had finished everything except vacuuming the upstairs. The minutes began to tick by and no Dan. With each passing second, I could feel the anger going up another notch. Then, my mind began its playing of the negative tapes. Bad resentful bitter thoughts raced through my head. With each stroke of the vacuum and each evil thought, the rage grew. By 5:15 P.M., I could hardly stand it. My burning head was ready to erupt like a volcano. I began vacuuming more quickly and vigorously.

I heard Dan drive up and come into the house. For a moment or two, I told myself, "Calm down, relax, get control." But as quickly as I thought it, I lost it. As hard as I tried to grasp for rationality, it was not within my reach. Becoming more frustrated, I pushed harder on the vacuum cleaner and waited fearfully for the explosion.

As Dan approached the top of the stairs, he looked at me with caution. He said, "I'm sorry I'm late. Let me help—I'll finish vacuuming." By that time, it was too late for me. I flew into a fit of rage—yelling, screaming, cursing - saying anything destructive that came to my mind.

Dan kept trying to talk to me calmly, explaining why he was late. But, it didn't matter what he said; I didn't have control of myself any longer. After several attempts of trying to take the vacuum from me to help out, I ordered Dan out of the house. My words were harsh and cruel, ugly and dirty.

After he left, I sat down on the carpet. My hands were shaking and I could feel my heart pounding. My mind was still racing, spinning, and dizzy. I looked at my watch. It was dinner time, and I had to pull myself together to get supper ready for Alexis.

As I was cooking, my mind continued playing its tricks on me. I would try to tell myself, "Calm down, let go of this, relax, call Dan and apologize." But as soon as that thought entered in, another more forceful negative voice said, "Don't give in, get even. Don't call, make him call you. Better yet, don't ever talk to him again—that will show him not to be late!"

My mind kept wavering back and forth like a see-saw. I began to feel dizzy again and somewhat faint. The phone began to ring. I was sure it was Dan—no way was I going to answer it.

After dinner, as I got Alexis ready for bed, the phone continued ringing and ringing. Inside my head, the noise of the ringing was intensifying with each call. Soon, it felt as though the ringing was in my head. At the same time, the negative tapes were playing over and over again, "Don't answer it, make him suffer. He hurt you, don't answer it."

I began to feel horribly frantic. I had to do something to stop the craziness. In the next moment I suddenly ran out of the bathroom (leaving Alexis in the empty tub) and madly pulled all the phone jacks out of the sockets. One by one, I jerked them out, and with the lessening of the noise level came the releasing of the siren in my head.

As my mind began to wind down, my body followed suit in the usual manner. I wanted to drop on the floor and cave in to the flood of emotions welling inside, but I had a young daughter to finish bathing and put to bed. I took a few deep breaths and climbed the stairs. Each step seemed monumental, but I kept my focus on Alexis.

Once I had tucked my little one in bed, I went to my bedroom. Looking at the phone jack on the floor, everything seemed so pathetic and so hopeless. I thought to myself, "What on earth is wrong with me? WHY must I go through this? Why can't I control IT; why does IT control me?"

I walked over to my bed and lay down. All the guilt, sadness, and shame that had built up inside me began to surface. I told myself, "You are really a worthless human being. You hurt the ones you love and who love you. You are not well—in fact you are crazy, yes, crazy."

The tears were uncontrollable. Thoughts of suicide entered by mind. Secretly, I had entertained suicide for some time, but every time I thought of my little girl, I was not able to carry it out. Even though I tried to hide as much of this darkness from her as possible, I wondered if she would not be better off without me. I chose to believe she wouldn't. I also wondered (and worried) about God. I had been told that suicide was definitely not in His plan for us, and if I chose that path, I could not spend eternity with Him. I was not willing to take that chance.

Nevertheless, the pain of worthlessness was almost unbearable. Through the tears, the scrambled mind, and the aching body, I mustered up my faith and said a prayer:

*Dear God,*

*Please forgive me for my anger, for my harsh words, and for my behaviors. Please forgive me for hurting my loved ones. Lord, help me. Please help me. I don't know what is wrong, but I do know I can't go on like this much longer. Please, Lord, show me. Guide me. Lead me. I will follow.*

The next morning I awoke feeling weary, but somewhat at peace. I tried to block out the ugly events from the night before and focus on this day. As I walked around and plugged in the phones, remorse and embarrassment tugged at me. I told myself I would call Dan and apologize.

Before I was able to call him, Dan called me. He asked me if I was all right, and told me he was worried because he tried to call many times, and there was no answer. I explained to him how and why I unhooked the phones. It seemed ridiculous retelling the events, but Dan did not judge me, he just listened. When I was done explaining and apologizing, Dan calmly apologized for being late. More importantly, he expressed his concern for me, reassured me he loved me, and thus, helped me in the process of reestablishing my self-worth. He knew how ashamed I felt, and he continually hammered in my head that the other Holli was a good person, a wonderful mother, and a loving wife-to-be.

A few days later when I was feeling myself (my menstrual period had begun), Dan sensitively suggested that I see a doctor. I flatly ruled out that idea. How could I explain to anyone what was going on without him or her confirming my greatest fear—that I was crazy! Dan dropped the idea for the time being, but in his eyes I could see the worry and the concern that he had for me.

"...It's a good day to be alive...it's a good day to be alive...it's a good..." my eyes are fixated on the napkin again. For me, today is a good day to be alive. I wish they all were. In fact, the past few days and even the past couple of weeks have been great. Being married again is wonderful; Dan is indeed a blessing.

After I finish breakfast and clean up the kitchen, I go upstairs to by bedroom to make the bed and straighten up the bathroom. As I am putting some clothes away in the closet, I glance down at my shoes. They are all in neat little rows, except for one or two. I bend down to put them into place. While lifting one shoe, an ugly memory comes to mind that had happened very recently. Tears surface quickly as the shame and guilt are still fresh from this episode. Sitting alone in the closet, I rethink the events of this occurrence and wonder to myself, "Why did this happen?"

It was a Saturday afternoon—a day to get all those chores done around the house that need attention. Although there was nothing in particular bothering me, I remember feeling anxious, irritable, and tense. I tried to focus on all the things that I needed to do, but whenever one insignificant thing went wrong, I could feel the tension building up inside me. For example, while simply putting clothes from the washer into the dryer, I would become nervous and irritated if one article of clothing dropped onto the floor!

I continued on throughout the day, feeling worse as time wore on. I wanted to do some ironing, but my hands were shaking so terribly that I wasn't able to hold the iron. Thinking that I was overdoing it, I sat down for a few minutes to glance through a magazine. Each time I tried to read a page, I could hardly focus on the words. The letters were sort of fuzzy. I rubbed my eyes, but it didn't help. I thought to myself, "This is strange. I have 20/20 vision." After moving the magazine towards and away from my face, I realized that it wasn't my eyes that were fuzzy, it was my mind that was unclear. I was not able to concentrate on any word long enough for my mind to register what the word was. My brain felt scattered and off course, like a bumper car jerking and ricocheting in every direction. I closed the magazine and tried to rest my eyes. As fatigued as I felt, there was a nervous energy within me that kept buzzing. For a moment I thought to myself, "This is really it. I am going crazy. I can't even think. I am losing my mind!"

I jumped up off the sofa and rushed upstairs. I had to keep busy, to stay focused, or else I might lose it all together. Cleaning the upstairs bathroom, I heard the front door open and close. I was sure it was Dan. I tried to relax, but I couldn't. I wanted to ask him to help me, but I was afraid. I wanted to tell him to go away and leave me alone, but I didn't really want that either. I gripped the edge of the counter and prepared for the explosion that was coming. Dan walked into the room and around the corner of the bathroom. He said something (I don't remember what); it wouldn't have mattered what it was anyway. I would have reacted the same way regardless of the subject. With the sound of his voice, the ANGER and RAGE that had been building all day began to unleash. I started screaming at him, yelling obscenities at the top of my lungs, and wildly accusing him of untruths. There was no use for Dan to try to defend himself; I was lost in my frenzy by this point.

Dan began to approach me to try calming me down, speaking softly and cautiously. It only infuriated me more. Feeling terribly desperate and frantic, I dashed into the closet to get away from him. Each word Dan spoke felt like another knife stabbing me and piercing my brain. Still yelling and crying at the same time, I searched with my eyes for something, anything to throw! Seeing the rows of shoes on the closet floor, I bent down and quickly began hurling them, one by one, at Dan.

For just a moment in this episode of frantic craziness, I was able to picture myself: a grown woman—a crying sobbing mess with hair hanging in her face and makeup running down it—on her hands and knees in a closet, throwing shoes at her husband. With just that flicker of reality, I let my body fall to the floor—the surge of incredible energy that I felt seconds before drained my body immediately. With my face in the carpet and my hands still grasping shoes, the ocean of

SORROW, SHAME, and DEPRESSION began to flow.

It seemed as though I lay there for hours. When the crying subsided, I tried to sit up. It felt as though I were paralyzed. My arms were heavy and weak at the same time. My head felt like it wobbled on my unsupportive neck. My fingers and hands ached from the clenching. I managed to pull myself up and walk over to the bed. I curled up in a fetal position holding my pillow in my arms. This time when the tears came, it was out of confusion, self-pity, and fear.

I felt too tired to pray. I didn't think it would help anyway. God had not answered my prayers. Nothing had changed—in fact, it had gotten worse. Those same old same old questions kept popping up in my mind.

Once again my thoughts drifted over to the option of suicide. Dan and Alexis deserved so much more than this. I pondered several different methods of how to do it, but I knew this was wrong. I thought of how much I loved them both and how much they loved me. It was something to hold on to.

When I awoke the next morning, Dan was lying beside me. He opened his eyes and motioned for me to come close. He wrapped his arms around me and held me tightly. With my head on his chest listening to his heart beat softly, I gave a quiet thanks to God for this wonderful man. For a long time, neither of us said a word. There was safety and healing in just being close.

Later that afternoon, when we did talk about what had happened, Dan expressed his same concerns. He wanted me to see a doctor, to talk to someone, to do something! He said it tore him apart to see me like that. There had to be a reason for all of it. But, I was so afraid and I didn't know who to turn to or where to go for help. Besides, there were so many days that I felt great. Things would get better, and I would just have to try harder.

Try harder...try harder... holding the shoe in my hand, I think about that as I put it into place. In that shoe episode, I did try harder, and nothing had happened! What would happen the next time? As I finish straightening the shoes and remain kneeling, I spend a quiet moment with

God.

*Heavenly Father,*

*Please forgive me for all the hurt I have caused my family and myself. Lord, I cannot do this anymore. I need you. I need your help. Please, take my life and make it worth living. Show me. Guide me. Lead me in your direction. I heard a song in church the other day that has stuck in my mind: "He who began a good work in you will be faithful to complete it." Father, please find that work in me and help to make it good. I believe that you can and that you will.*

# Hope and Help

Waiting in a doctor's office is not my idea of having fun! But, I'm here and I'm too self-conscious to get up and leave. Besides, it has taken so much to get myself here; I can't turn back now. Looking around the room, which has been pleasantly decorated in soothing mauve colors, I glance at the other women who casually look through the magazines on babies and various aspects of womanhood. I wonder if any of them are here for the same reason I am—but then, I'm not really sure of what that reason is myself. A very dear friend of mine, Pat, has recommended that I come here. I remember our conversation from a few weeks past.

Pat and I teach at the same junior high school. A few years ago, I was fortunate enough to have her daughter in my eighth grade English and History class. She was a special student whom I got to know quite well. Even after she graduated from eighth grade, Pat kept me posted on her daughter's well-being. I came to learn that her daughter suffered with some very serious physical and psychological problems. Pat had closely monitored her daughter's declining health and she sought out several doctors in search of help and treatment. In Pat's frustration with finding appropriate care for her daughter, she would often come to me and describe what was taking place.

As I became more aware and involved with Pat's daughter's condition, a strange but ironic thing happened. As Pat would describe the physical and emotional turmoil that her daughter was going through, I felt as though Pat were describing me. The irrational behaviors that she described—RAGE, extreme ANXIETY, deep DEPRESSION, and feelings of WORTHLESSNESS—were so familiar, in fact, second nature, to me.

Finally, after months of talking with Pat, I decided to get up the courage to tell her that I too suffered many of the same problems that her daughter did. I was so frightened. "What would she think of me? Would she think I was crazy?"

I told myself, "No, Pat is such a good friend; she wouldn't pass judgement on me. She would help me—just as she was trying to help her own daughter."

One day at school, as I was thinking about approaching Pat, she told me she had some great news to share with me. Before I said anything about my situation, Pat excitedly told me about a physician in town to whom she had taken her daughter. She shared with me that she thought she had found (or at least was on to) the cause of her daughter's physical and psychological problems! The doctor who had examined Pat's daughter, thoroughly and completely, diagnosed the problem as a serious but treatable illness—Premenstrual Syndrome (PMS).

Although Pat's daughter had just begun treatment, Pat felt very confident about the physician and program of care that had been prescribed. I couldn't believe what I was hearing! Pat's daughter wasn't crazy! (Could that mean I wasn't crazy either?) There was actually an explanation, a reason, a cause for her pain. Tears welled in my eyes as I felt a feeling of relief for Pat's daughter and a flicker of hope for myself.

With relative ease, I shared with Pat my secret. She did not act at all surprised and was of course, nonjudgemental. She immediately took on her motherly role and informed me that I had better get on the phone and make an appointment immediately to see this doctor.

Oh! Someone just called my name. I look up at the reception desk and the nurse asks me to fill out a form regarding insurance matters. I get the papers, sit back down, and begin filling out the required information. As I get to the part that asks for marital status, I still feel awkward checking off "Married" and writing down a new last name. As I continue filling out the form, I keep telling myself, "Maybe you should leave. What if you don't have PMS? What if you are just plain crazy? What if they laugh at you?" I want to go, but for some reason I don't. I finish the forms, return them to the desk, and sit back down.

A few moments later, the nurse calls my name and motions for me to follow her. After taking my weight and height measurements, she has me sit down in a comfortable, quiet room. For at least twenty minutes or more, the nurse carefully takes a complete medical history. When questioning me about my menstrual cycle, the nurse asks me about some areas that are extremely difficult for me to answer. It's not that I do not know the answers, it's that my responses seem shameful and are embarrassing. She would ask me if I ever got terribly angry, if I felt "out-of-control," if I was deeply depressed, or if I ever thought of suicide. I answer as honestly as I can. Surprisingly, the nurse does not seem taken aback by anything that I say; in fact, frequently, she looks up at me and nods with an air of understanding and compassion. As the nurse continues to jot down everything I say, I secretly pray to God. I pray that today will bring answers, perhaps even solutions to my problems. I pray that I am in the right place.

When we are done, the nurse takes me into the examining room. She instructs me to undress completely and she informs me that the doctor will be in shortly. As I sit on the examination table wrapped up in the hard, rough, white paper gown, I feel so afraid. I have lived with this *thing* for so long; maybe it is "just me." I begin to feel nervous and sweaty, I wish I could get dressed and leave. The seconds tick by ever so slowly—minutes seem like hours.

The door opens. In walks a vibrant, attractive young woman with a huge smile on her face. The room seems to fill with her energy and her warmth. She takes my hand, holds it gently, and introduces herself as Marcia. I am immediately put at ease with her presence.

Marcia begins the examination with a complete physical, including blood and lab work (to rule out other conditions). After she is done, Marcia sits down next to me and we begin to discuss psychological symptoms. As we discuss the bouts of depression, the rage, the hysteria, Marcia seems to know, and better yet, to understand, exactly what I am describing. Most surprisingly, she is not shocked by what I have to say.

When the examination period is done, Marcia carefully instructs me to do a couple of things. I am to begin taking a multi-vitamin, and I am to chart my symptoms (menstrual cycle disorders, moods, depression, weight gain, as well as other physical and psychological disorders) over the next three months. Marcia gives me a specific format to follow, so that the charting will be done accurately and thoroughly.

Although I feel somewhat discouraged (I guess I had hoped for an immediate cure), Marcia is kind and empathetic in her words, "I don't know if you have PMS. We will find out. Whatever the problem is, we will confront it and treat it."

As Marcia leaves the room, my emotions are mixed. I seem to trust her implicitly already, but I am very afraid. I think "What if I don't have PMS? And, even if I do, what can she do for me? How much longer will I have to suffer like this? How much more can my family endure?"

A little voice in my mind says, "Trust Me, trust Me."

*******

Well, here I am again, waiting in a doctor's office. This time, however, I am not as afraid, just anxious. It has been three months since I was last here. I have done everything that Marcia has asked me to do. I have followed her instructions to the T. I have carefully charted my behaviors, emotions, and physical symptoms. I have taken the vitamins regularly. Unfortunately, in the past three months, there has been no difference; in fact, in many ways, I have felt worse. I continue to feel as though I am losing my grip on reality. I sit nervously and wait, wondering what Marcia will say and do. A few moments later, the nurse directs me to an examination room. As I sit staring at my charts, Marcia gracefully enters the room.

Again, her smile is warm and reassuring. We talk at great length about the past three months, and Marcia methodically studies my charts. Together, we distinguish some distinct repetitive patterns in my symptoms. She thoroughly and carefully outlines the pattern of symptoms and she explains their relationship with my menstrual cycle. This information, along with the additional blood and lab work (which came back normal), confirm Marcia's suspicions.

Marcia shares with me that she believes that I do suffer from Pre-menstrual Syndrome, and in fact, my case is quite acute. As she shares this information, I cannot control the tears. These are not tears of pity, or shame, or nonsense. They are tears of pure relief. Marcia gives me a hug and as I quietly ask myself, and as I quietly ask myself, "You mean, I am not crazy?" Marcia hears my small cry. Her response is unbelievable to me, "So many, many, women like yourself are asking themselves that same question. They suffer just as you do. And just as you have kept it quiet for so many years, so have they. Physicians are just now willing to learn more about PMS and to treat it effectively. We have a long way to go in the medical field in finding a cure, but we have a program here that I believe can help you tremendously. Whatever you do, don't let anyone tell you that your problems are all in your head or that your PMS is just a convenient excuse to act irrationally. You and I know that no woman would choose any degree of PMS over a consistent, stable, sane state of mind."

As my relief and joy continue to spin around inside of me, I try to concentrate as Marcia writes down and explains a plan of treatment. She instructs me to do several things: 1)continue my vitamins and double the amount with the onset of ovulation, 2)watch my diet very carefully and refrain from specific foods on a list she provides, 3)exercise regularly, 4)reduce stress whenever possible (especially with the onset of ovulation), and 5)get plenty of rest (especially when the mood swings begin to intensify). I am instructed to follow this plan for the next three months, along with continuing to chart my physical and psychological symptoms.

Although I am excited about the program, I feel somewhat let down. In my own selfish way, I want an easier, instant cure! This is going to take time, concentrated effort, and a willingness on my part (even when I don't feel like it) to follow all of these instructions. I am also afraid, "What if I do all this and nothing happens? What will I do next?"

Marcia senses my frustration and we discuss it. She reassures me that she is very confident that I will see results over the next few months, but she agrees with me that it will take a strong commitment on my part. I must do exactly as she says, every day, without fail. Before I leave, Marcia adds something that encourages me just a little. "Holli, if you start to feel extremely depressed, or find that you already are, I want you to call the office. I am going to have you come in and give you a progesterone injection. This might help to stabilize your emotions." Then Marcia goes on to explain what progesterone is and how it relates to PMS.[1]

Driving away from the office, my mind reviews all that has been said. For the first time, I feel a flicker of hope. Something tugs at my heart. I look up into the sky as I am driving, "Yes, God, You are there. I thank you for directing me to Marcia. I thank You for her knowledge of PMS and her ability to treat women. Thank You for answering my prayer." I chuckle inside as a little voice says, "I told you so. Trust Me next time, will 'ya?"

*******

Another three months has passed, more quickly than I realize. As I wait to see Marcia, I am anxious to share

---

[1] Today, progesterone intra-muscular injections are usually no longer given due to the development of rectal suspensions, rectal/vaginal suppositories and oral capsules.

some good news for a change! Although there is a long way to go, I have had an improved three months. I have done everything that marcia had asked me to do. My family was incredibly supportive. Dan helped by always laying out my vitamins and by watching my chart with me to allow for more rest and exercise when needed. And, having explained, in simple terms, about PMS and what it had to do with me, Alexis became a fantastic little helper as well. They both encouraged me at all times. There were several occasions when the depression was more than I could handle, and, as Marcia had instructed me to do, I went to the office for progesterone injections. They gave me tremendous relief and some stability, during those dark times.

The nurse takes me into the examination room and Marcia follows closely behind. It amazes me how positive and alive Marcia always seems to be. I look forward to seeing her joyful face.

After a few minutes of friendly talk, Marcia and I again look over my charts and discuss the past three months. We are both thrilled at the progress that has been made. However, Marcia, as well as I, would like more of a consistency in that improvement. As I explain it in my own words to Marcia, "I want to feel as though I am in control of the PMS, rather than it controlling me."

Marcia knows exactly what I am saying. She explains that this will come with time, and perhaps, with something else as well. Marcia explains that she would like to start me on "progesterone treatment." First of all, she gives me a thorough background on the hormone, its pro's and con's, and how it relates to PMS and its treatment. Marcia suggests that I begin using rectal suspension (a liquid progesterone inserted through the rectum), to be taken once a day starting with the onset of ovulation and continuing through to the first signs of the menstrual flow. I recall the relief I felt from the few injections I had already received, and I heartily agree. At the same time, I am to continue with all other aspects of the treatment program.

Marcia wants me to begin this therapy and continue for the next six months. Unless I have any setbacks or problems, I don't have to return to the doctor's office for six months. She encourages me to call, however, if I have any concerns or worries. I tell her I'll miss her—she's become more than a doctor to me—she is a dear friend.

As I leave the office that day, the hope that I have felt before seems to sparkle just a bit brighter this time. Before I start my car, I bow my head:

*Heavenly Father,*

*Thank you for helping me—for saving my life. Forgive me for not trusting you more fully and completely. Lord, please continue to guide me and direct me. Show me what to do and where to go. More than anything, I want to be a well and whole woman, physically and emotionally. Most importantly, I want to be the woman that You would have me to be.*

# Hard Work

Oh, good heavens! It's almost 6:15 P.M. I need to hurry up. I finish part of my dinner, excuse myself from the table, and apologize to Dan and Alexis for leaving them with the mess in the kitchen. I have just about thirty minutes to get ready to attend a get-together for a group of people who have been working diligently all year for a special cause at our junior high school.

As I climb the stairs, I think about this group of people and how hard they have worked. I, too, have put in many hours. For the past seven years (since 1980), I have taught gifted and talented students in the areas of English and history. In addition to teaching, I have also become politically active in the controversy that surrounds gifted and talented education. Although this has been a very time consuming and challenging issue to tackle, it has also been an extremely rewarding one.

While I'm putting on my make-up and am looking closely into the mirror, I see a different Holli than I saw a year ago. Even though I would have gone to this gathering a year ago, or even five years ago, I wouldn't have felt the same about myself as I do tonight.

Just recently, for the first time in some many, many years, I have experienced what it is like to feel good about myself. Having lost my self-worth so long ago, it is foreign, but wonderful, to feel valuable again. This, too, has not come easily. It has taken a lot of hard work, communication, and prayer. Much of my gain I owe to yet another valuable individual.

For the past six months or so, I have been seeing a counselor. Her name is Sherri. She is not just any counselor, but one who specializes in treating women with PMS. My friend, Pat, recommended Sherri to me when Pat witnessed how much Sherri had helped her daughter.

I was reluctant, at first, to go to a counselor. After all, Marcia was doing all that she could to help me, and I was feeling so much better. In fact, each month seemed to bring greater stability and balance into my life. However, there was still room for improvement.

As I began visiting and talking with Sherri, I was amazed at the many areas in my life that the PMS has infected. Not only had the PMS affected me as a person, but it had also impacted my relationships with my husband and daughter as well as with family and friends. In addition, because I had lived with PMS for so long, I had instinctively developed behaviors that helped me to deal with the illness, but unfortunately, they were neither positive nor productive.

The first area that Sherri and I worked on was me. She helped me to understand that I, like most women with PMS, believe that we are the source of our problem, not the illness. After experiencing years of self-punishment and guilt, it is extremely difficult to differentiate between the two. By recognizing that fact alone, my healing in this area could begin.

Sherri pointed out something to me, at this point in our counseling, that was invaluable. Although I did not know if Sherri was a Christian or not, she knew that I was. She suggested to me that I spend time in prayer—asking for forgiveness for myself and others I had hurt), for cleansing (a releasing of all the ugly, negative thoughts and feelings about myself), and for strength (to be able and willing to change my thinking about myself). In my heart, I knew that only through God would I be able to do these things; I could never accomplish them by myself. I began to make it a routine part of my prayer time.

The second area that Sherri and I tackled was relationships. Sherri encouraged Dan to attend some of the sessions and he did. I was shocked, but not angry, at some of his fears and anxieties. I had never fully realized what an impact my PMS had on him. Dan had always been so supportive of me that I hadn't recognized that he too was being hurt by this illness, and he needed support as well. Sherri helped us to communicate our feelings more effectively to one another about the PMS, and she demonstrated how each of us could help the other, especially during those difficult times. For example, Dan and I learned that during one of my fits of rage, it was best for him not to say anything to me. As difficult as that may be for him, it would help me. We also discovered that when I was deeply depressed, just having Dan hold me tightly and closely brought great comfort, even if I insisted that I wanted to be alone. In turn, I was able to help Dan in little ways that also brought him comfort. One very simple but needed task was verbally reassuring Dan that he was not the source of my unhappiness, but in fact, it was he who helped bring me out of darkness many times. Giving him cute cards or little notes that expressed my love and appreciation for him brought him much relief, especially when I was very depressed and didn't feel like talking.

Although Dan was the primary recipient of the hurt inflicted from my PMS, Alexis had also received her share. Even though Alexis was still a young child, Sherri encourage me to talk to her about PMS. Sherri explained how important it was to let Alexis know that she was not the source or cause of my anger, depression, or other negative behaviors related to my PMS. It was also important that I ask not only for her understanding and patience, but for her forgiveness as well. Again, through communication, healing could begin, it would take time and effort, but I knew that Alexis was ready and willing.

In my other relationships with family and friends, I knew that I too must forgive myself and ask those I had hurt for their forgiveness. I could not necessarily expect them to go out of their way to help me, but what Sherri taught me to do was to explain briefly to those close to me what PMS was and how I was attempting to reshape my life.

The third area of improvement was in changing the negative behaviors that I had developed in reaction to what I was feeling through the effects of PMS. This has been and still is the most difficult area to change. Again, because I had suffered from PMS for so much of my life, theses uncontrollable behaviors were my only way of coping. Sherri and I discussed these behaviors and ways to fight them off before they could overtake me. More and more, I began to understand that once the PMS had reached a critical point physically and psychologically, I could and would lose the control that I so desperately needed. I had to learn and practice these coping techniques while I was in a PMS-free period in my cycle so that I would be prepared when the dark times would strike!

This has taken incredible concentration, energy, and willingness. It has been painfully difficult because, as I realize that these behaviors must change in order for my life to be in balance, I also face the feeling that I am not a worthy or a good person. The poor-me tapes play in my mind and negative thoughts try to flood my brain. Over and over again, I have to say to myself that it isn't me that's the problem, it's the PMS. Then I can use my new techniques for coping with the problem.

There are various coping techniques that I have tried. I never give up. Some days one works when others don't. For example, when I feel the rage starting to build inside of me, I physically try to remove myself from whatever I am doing at the moment or just stop whatever I am doing and take deep, long breaths. While I am taking deep breaths, I force myself to think of something, anything, positive. Another example is when I begin to feel anxious, nervous, and extremely irritable. I look at my schedule and what I am trying to get accomplished. I try to cut down or eliminate some of the chores, or activities, or obligations. Or, I simply tell myself to slow down or calm down; and then, I have to repeat it over and over again.

One of the best techniques has been communication with my family. When I begin to enter into the cycle of the month where I can feel myself changing, I simply forewarn Dan and Alexis that I am not feeling myself. This is NOT an excuse for me to act irrationally. It is a positive signal to them that allows them to help me better, and it is a confirmation to me that I must really be on guard.

As I am driving home later that evening, I can't wait to tell Dan my news. He will be so proud of me. I pull into the driveway and park the car. I hop out and dash into the house. Dan is waiting in the living room. I walk over to him, trying to hide the smile on my face, but it is hard. He asks me, "What are you hiding behind your back?" Without wasting a moment more, I show him the lovely engraved clipboard that the parents on the committee have given me for all my work in gifted and talented education. I tell Dan of the touching words and comments that were said about me. Tears of happiness fill my eyes. Dan responds in his usual positive manner. "Of course, what else do you expect them to say about a great teacher?" He gives me a big hug. "I'm proud of you, honey."

That night, as I get ready for bed, I feel as though I am on cloud nine. Lying on bed, I close my eyes for a moment with God.

*Dear Lord,*

*There is so much to be thankful for—my family, my friends, my co-workers, Sherri, and of course, You. I know I am not over PMS. But, I feel as though I finally have a handle on it. I also thank You for making that song that I love come true for me: "He who began a good work in you will be faithful to complete it."*

As my eyes become heavy and I drift into a deep solid sleep, I seem to vaguely hear Him say, "I'm not through with you yet."

# Darkness Returns

I anxiously wait. I keep looking through the small crowd of people, searching for Dan. The rather stunted-looking airplane is carrying more passengers than I had thought possible. There he is. He is bending down to get through the doorway of the aircraft, looking as handsome as always.

As I anticipate his hug and kiss, I think about what a wonderful weekend we have in store for us. I have rented a house at Pajaro Dunes (my favorite place at the beach), and Dan and I are going to have a quiet couple of days together. Alexis and I have spent the past week together at this beautiful spot of ours, and now she is with her dad enjoying some quality time with him.

Here he comes. Even though I have not been away from Dan for long, I have missed him more than he knows. I've had time over the past week to think over the year and I have so much to share with him.

I wave my hand and he sees me. He walks over and just holds me for a moment. His strong arms feel wonderful around my back. His gentle kiss on my forehead suddenly makes me seem totally at home with him.

Driving from Monterey Airport over to Pajaro Dunes doesn't take long and the scenery is absolutely picturesque. The assorted, tall, green pines fill the air with a freshness that Dan and I both love, and the cool overcast breeze brings us comfort from the scorching heat of the desert summer months. I think Dan enjoys the beach at Pajaro Dunes almost as much as I do—for along with its peacefulness, solitude, and beauty, it also brings back pleasant memories of some very special times together.

After getting Dan unpacked and settled in, we take

a walk along the clean, solitary beach. As we let our feet melt into the wet sand and surf and with our arms clasped tightly around one another against the cool ocean breeze, I think back for a moment on all the changes we have made over the past year. It almost seems like a bad dream.

At the end of the 1987 school year, Dan had an offer from his brother, Jim, to join his pool cleaning business that he had established in the Palm Springs area. After much prayer, a two week practice run for Dan at the new career, and God taking care of all the obstacles that could have stood in our way, Dan and I made this gigantic change in our life.

After selling our house, Dan, Alexis, Pebbles(our dog), and I tearfully said good-bye to our family and friends, our home, our church, our co-workers, and our life in Stockton. With only our faith to guide us, we drove five hundred miles away from everything that was familiar and safe.

Because I had been hired for a teaching position in Hemet, a small town approximately an hour from Palm Desert, Dan, Alexis and I decided it would be best to live there, at least for the time being, while Dan commuted to the desert. And, because we weren't sure what kind of income Dan would be earning, we moved in with Dan's dad in order to make things easier financially.

Putting all our belongings, except for clothing, into storage, Dan, Alexis and I moved in with "Brick," my father-in-law. Shortly after we settled in, my step-son, who was fifteen, came to live with us. The five of us lived in a two bedroom, furniture-filled, older home, with several of today's modern conveniences lacking. To add to the stresses of an extremely crowded living situation and adjusting to our new teen-aged family member I had a very unpleasant teaching assignment in a disorganized and out-of-control middle school. Dan had a long commute, twice a day, after challenging days of learning and adjusting to an entirely different career. On top of that was the loneliness of knowing absolutely no one in a town that catered primarily to the elderly or the retired. We existed this way for an entire year.

"Holli, Holli, come on, what are you thinking? You are in such deep thought. Let me in on it!"

Dan grabs my side and starts to tickle me. It's one of his favorite ways of getting my attention, or helping me to snap out of those too serious thoughts. I tell him it's nothing; he knows that is not true. But, he lets it go for now, just enjoying the peacefulness of the moment.

Before we get too cold from our walk along the beach, we return to the condominium to fix dinner. I have bought some steaks to barbecue, some red potatoes, artichokes and makings for salad. As I'm slicing the tomatoes, I accidentally cut my finger. It's nothing serious, but it does require a good rinsing and a bandage. Dan looks for first aid supplies while I stand running the cold water over the cut. Looking down at the blood, I think of an incident that happened not too long ago when the emotional pain lasted much longer and was much more severe than the sting from the small cut on my finger. I shamefully recall the ugly episode.

Dan and I were on our way out to dinner on a Saturday night. It was a special time for the two of us. Saturday nights were really our only time alone together. We looked forward to those evenings as a time of relaxation and communication for both of us.

Unfortunately, on this Saturday evening, I was not feeling like myself at all. The week had been filled with the stresses of the overcrowded living conditions, problems at work, financial worries, and extreme loneliness. On top of that, the PMS symptoms (both physical and psychological) were getting the better of me. Instead of avoiding any topics which could ignite an immediate rage in me, I chose to dwell on all the negative things I could think of.

As Dan and I were driving over to the restaurant, we began to argue. Or should I say that I began to complain about everything and anything? Whatever suggestion Dan would make or however he approached a problem made no difference. All I wanted to do was strike and strike hard. Within a few blocks I was yelling, crying and cursing. Because Dan was so exhausted from his week of grueling work, his fuse was short. He began firmly responding to my irrational remarks, but all that did was anger me more. I thought to myself, "Where are his comforting words? Doesn't he care? Who does he think he is, criticizing me?" My anger grew into irrational madness. I knew where I could hurt him the most.

I started to attack him verbally. Any mean or degrading comment that would flash into my sick mind, I would throw out at him. When Dan had listened to enough, he calmly but loudly told me that I was a sick person. These words burned in my head. I felt like I was going to burst with rage. My eyes were wildly searching for something, anything, to lash out to and then...I couldn't stand it any longer. While I was screaming and sobbing, I took my hands and started to hit Dan as hard as I could. He stopped the car and held up his arms to block the blows. Even with the adrenalin flowing rapidly within me, my strength was no match to Dan's and I quickly realized that I was physically hurting myself more than Dan. Even though my hands began to ache, my mind would not allow me to let go of the anger. I kept asking myself, "What else can I do to hurt him? What else can I do?"

Suddenly, I reached for the car door. It had been raining outside and it was cold, but I didn't care. While continuing on with my verbal onslaught, I opened the door, pulled myself out of the car, and slammed the door behind me. I started walking briskly down the street, not knowing where I was or where I was going. I thought to myself, "This will show Dan. This will really get to him. He will feel really bad for me and he will come and apologize."

A few moments later, Dan drove up slowly and followed along the side of me for just a moment. When I wouldn't turn my head to acknowledge him, he drove off! As he drove away, I stood there in disbelief. As it started to drizzle, I could feel my body and my mind starting to unwind.

I wanted to sit down, or even lie down, on the sidewalk. but it was too wet. I could feel the exhaustion and the depression begin to set in. Within moments, the warm tears came flowing freely from my eyes. As the rain washed them from my cheeks I looked up at the dark sky and questioned God. I knew that this was not His fault or my punishment, but I couldn't understand why this was happening when I was still doing everything that Marcia had instructed me to do.

Before long Dan returned and parked the car next to the sidewalk. Shakily, I walked over and climbed in. Quietly, we drove to the restaurant. Before we got out, I looked down at my stinging hands. I saw the cuts, the dripping blood and the swelling. My rain coat was blood stained and my face was blotchy from crying.

When we finally walked inside the restaurant, I immediately went to the ladies' room to clean up. I fixed my hair and make-up and rinsed off my hands. The swelling was still pretty bad but I would have to make do.

Dan and I ordered dinner. We kept fairly silent. Dan didn't know what to say and I didn't know how to say it. When our dinner arrived, Dan said grace and then reached over to take my plate. He cut the steak up into small pieces for me. He knew that my hands were too sore and swollen to cut it myself, but he also knew that I was too ashamed to admit it.

As I watched him cut my meat, my eyes filled with tears. A short time ago, I was screaming awful things at this man I loved so dearly, and yet, he still cared for me. He never gave up on me. I knew I mustn't either.

"Here you go, honey, I found this small bandage in the master bathroom. This should do it." Dan dries off the cut and carefully places the dressing around it. I continue finishing up the salad and artichokes. Dan helps with the potatoes and barbecues the steaks.

We sit down at the dining room table next to the window over-looking the ocean. The smell of the moist air, the sound of the waves crashing and the seagulls calling, and the sight of the endless ocean seems to wash away yesterday's struggles. With our hands clasped tightly, Dan and I give thanks to our Father for all our many blessings.

That night, before I fall asleep, I think about the past year in more detail. As I struggle to put the pieces of the puzzle together as to why things fell apart this year, I concentrate on how they fell apart. When I think of the one word that best describes the year, I think of "depressing." I quickly recall how that depression manifested itself in me. In fact, it totally dominated my life.

Getting through the work week was much easier than the weekend. Teaching, shopping, cooking, cleaning, and helping Alexis with homework, plus spending some time with her, took up most of the day and part of the night. Once Dan arrived home, we had dinner, watched a little TV, and then we all went to bed.

One thing that I vividly remember was that each night before dinner, I would have one or two glasses of wine. Although this does not sound like much, for me, it was. It was enough to numb the homesickness and emptiness that ached inside of me. Also, the wine made me very tired, and I was able to sleep quite well. I know that even though it was a small amount, I became dependent on that feeling, and each day I looked forward to numbing myself again.

The weekends were, at times, unbearable. Dan and his son would get up very early (4:30 A.M.), and drive to the desert so that Dan could get home in time to go out to dinner. When I would awake Saturday morning, I didn't want to get out of bed. Many times, depending on how I was feeling with the PMS, I would just lie in bed for hours, crying. It would take every bit of effort that I could muster up to simply get up, shower, get dressed, and do the grocery shopping. If fact, if it hadn't been for Alexis and her kind and patient words, I doubt that I would have gotten up at all.

After the grocery shopping was done, Alexis and I would vacuum, dust, and straighten up the house. As I would work my way through the rooms which were incredibly cluttered with "old folks" memorabilia, I would find myself becoming increasingly resentful and angry at the situation I was in. Each time I had to juggle furniture or dishes or towels around just so that I could get to something that I needed, I became frustrated and depressed. Sometimes, with each chair that I lifted or each dresser drawer that I rearranged, I would actually feel the life draining out of me.

I remember one day in particular when everything seemed so

hopeless. Alexis and I had just hung all the laundry out to dry on the lines (there was no dryer) when it started to rain. We ran out and took all the clothing and towels down. After about twenty minutes, the rain stopped so we hung all the laundry back up again. No sooner had we finished than it started to rain once more. I wanted to give up, I just didn't care.

After Alexis and I had finished with our work, there was really nothing for us to do. We knew no one. These were the difficult times, the dark times. Many times, I thought of running away. I just wanted to pack some things, take Alexis, and leave. I wanted to escape all the unhappiness I felt.

As badly as I wanted to leave, Somehow I knew that it would only make matters worse. I thought about how hard Dan was working in order to get home so that we could go out to dinner together. I thought about the fact that I, too, had made the decision to move away from "home," And that I had no right to blame Dan or others. However, I continued to play negative tapes in my head, feel sorry for myself, and to dig a deeper hole of depression.

Depression...depression...depression...yes, that is indeed the best word to describe my state of mind for the past year. Before I close my eyes I talk to God:

*Heavenly Father,*

*I am not sure as to all the why's of this very difficult past year. Are they so obvious that I can't see them or are they to remain hidden from me? Am I to continue to live like this forever? I really thought that I had this PMS thing under control, but it's worse than ever. I don't understand. I know I have not gone to church very much lately, and I have not been reading the Bible as I should. Are You mad at me? I am sorry for not praying regularly or for including You more in my life. I hope that You will forgive me. Please Father, do not give up on me...do not give up on me...do not gi....*

\*\*\*\*\*\*\*

"Good morning, sweetheart! It's a beautiful day to be alive."

I can hardly believe my ears. What time is it, anyway? Dan enters the bedroom whistling as loudly as he can. How can anyone be so happy first thing in the morning? He brings me a cup of coffee to help break the shock.

After Dan spends his usual time torturing me with tickling that almost makes me cry, I am then more than ready to get up and greet the day. We shower, get dressed, eat a small breakfast, and head for the tennis courts. Dan beats me terribly, according to the score, but I remind him that my technique is really much better than his strength. Still, I am not a very good loser, and we decide to head for the beach for an afternoon of relaxation.

The sun peeks through the clouds and overcast sky. It's just enough to keep the coolness from being uncomfortable. Secretly, I would like it a bit warmer, but Dan is in heaven. Lying on the sand, we drift in and out of sleep. The ocean crashes a short distance away, and the ever-present seagulls swoop and call, swoop and call.

Some time later, Dan and I open our eyes almost simultaneously. With our heads facing, one ear to the sand and one to the sky, and with a welcome blanket pulled up around our shoulders, we begin to talk.

I share with Dan how I am afraid of the depression and what it has done to me, to us, and to the family. He listens intently and at length. I express my frustration with all that I have done and am trying to do to get the PMS under control. I tell him I feel I am waging a losing battle. I regretfully reveal the shame, embarrassment, and guilt that I carry for the irrational behaviors that I have been unable to control. I cry as I begin to acknowledge those feelings of total self-worthlessness that have begun to manifest themselves within me again. When I am done, Dan looks at me calmly and lovingly, and he speaks.

He begins by reassuring me of his unconditional love. Then, in his analytical, but caring, way, he outlines what he sees as the reasons for all the depression. First of all, he points out to me that I always put far too many expectations on myself (being the perfect teacher, the best wife, the super mom, etc.). Secondly, Dan reminds me of what Sherri had shared with both of us, "Whenever possible, reduce stress, especially during a PMS time." Dan begins to list, one by one, all the stresses we encountered and lived through the past year (changing jobs, moving, living in crowded conditions, new family members, homesickness, and so on). Thirdly, Dan questions me about my walk with God and where I am in my relationship with Him. Have I stayed close to Him? Has my prayer life been active? Has He been first in my life?

Just listening to Dan, the cloud of confusion in my mind seems to clear. There is an incredible sense of relief as I start to process the thought that once again I am not the source of the problem. Somewhere, somehow, someway, during the long dark days of this past year, I lost fact of that one crucially important fact.

Tears well up and run down my face. Dan wipes them with his sandy hand, but his touch feels good. He draws me close and I bury my face in his soft, warm shirt. For the moment, I feel safe and at peace. As the grief releases itself from my body, Dan holds me tightly. Hidden in my sobs, I ask God to find that "good work" in me, to dig down deep within my soul and bring it out. I tell Him that this time I won't take for granted that the work is done. I tell Him that I am ready for it to be a never-ending job.

# Pieces Of The Puzzle

Thirty-some-odd desks are scattered about the rather small fabricated classroom—even the chalk board looks temporary. The teacher's desk is nestled between the back wall and the first so-called row of desks. I have chosen the first seat in the middle of the room, about one foot from where the professor will teach. I have come prepared—prepared to learn a lot! This class, Analysis and Explication of Poetry, is going to be a challenging one. I have had this professor before. He is demanding, he expects nothing less than one's best, but he will teach me more than most all of my previous professors put together. As I sit in this sterile chilly room, I look around at the other students—some older, some younger— and I wonder why they are here.

I am here because I have no choice. I was informed a year ago that I had been teaching English under a teaching credential that really did not permit me to teach at the junior high or high school level. If I wanted to continue teaching eighth grade, I had to return to school and complete the necessary courses in order to obtain the needed supplementary credential.

So, here I am. This is the last of the three courses that I have needed to take, and then I will be done. In spite of all the homework, papers, mid-terms, and finals. I have experienced tremendous growth in my life—intellectually, physically, psychologically, and spiritually.

"Oh, I'm sorry. Did you say something to me?" As usual, I'm off in my deep-thought land and the young man next to me has asked me my name and if I live in Palm Desert. I briefly explain to him that my husband, daughter, and I moved to Palm Desert from Hemet last summer. I explain that my husband has a pool-cleaning business here in the desert, and that I teach eighth grade English at a middle school in Indio. He asks me why I am taking this class and I explain my circumstances. I learn that his name is Ed, he lives in Palm Desert, and that he is an ex-pastor returning to school to obtain his teaching credential.

We continue to talk for a short time. Ed asks me if I know anything about Doug, the professor, and I share about the class that I had taken with him before and how grateful I am for having him again. I hesitate for a moment and think about what I just said. Yes, I am grateful for Doug. For, if it had not been for Doug, I would not have made the choices that I did while in his class. I wouldn't have discovered the information that I did, and I certainly wouldn't have felt comfortable sharing that information with just anyone. I reflect about how absolutely amazing God has been. He has put every single piece of the puzzle together every single time.

I picture myself sitting in the Assistant Superintendent's office of the new school district which was about to hire me. I remember distinctly this very large bold man telling me that he would love to hire me, but that I didn't have the appropriate credentials. I was in shock! I was angry, and I was confused. I thought to myself, "How can this be? I have been teaching this level for eight years!" After hearing the disturbing news, this man's secretary informed me that I could teach the ensuing year under an emergency credential, but that I would have to go back to school and obtain another credential if I wished to continue teaching at the junior high level. Still upset, I agreed to do so—I really had no choice.

When I went home after the interview, I was even more angry and resentful. I just couldn't understand why. After having such a difficult year in Hemet with all the stresses, Dan and I agreed that we were going to take it easier this year and do everything possible to keep the stress levels down. We had taken some positive steps in that direction. We had moved from Hemet, bought a nice home in Palm Desert, reunited ourselves with all our belongings, found a wonderful church, and we were making friends with some caring supportive people. Still, there were the challenges of a new job in a new school for me, a new school for Alexis, Dan's growing business, and readjusting our family unit again (my step-son moved back to Stockton to be with his family and friends).

After discussing the situation with Dan, I felt much better. We agreed that I would not start school until the winter quarter. That would give me time to adjust to our new routines and to prepare for my teaching. During this time, my PMS was not as bad as it had been in Hemet, but I was still discouraged because I knew that I could be feeling even better. Many times, I thought about calling Marcia. Stupidly, I didn't. I thought she might be disappointed in me that I wasn't doing well, and secretly, I was ashamed and guilt-ridden about my regression.

The fall quarter went by quickly, and before I knew it, I was registering for my first class. I groaned inside as I learned it was to be Advanced Composition. I knew this meant lots and lots of writing! "Where was I going to find the time? When was I going to be able to do research?" The worries began to build inside me.

The first night of class, my anxieties were far from alleviated. Doug, the professor, walked in, took roll, informed us of his expectations, and then proceeded to tell us that approximately one-third of us would not pass his class. Although this frightened me somewhat, it also served as a great motivator. I was not about to flunk out!

As the weeks wore on, I was extremely busy writing, editing, rewriting, and completing the written assignments. Doug gave us a variety of challenging types of essays from which to choose, and he always kept the topics open. This allowed the students to be comfortable with their subject matter, and it also opened the door for Doug to get to know each of us on a more personal level.

I began to see Doug in a little different light as well. Although his expectations remained extremely high, I could tell that he was a sensitive and caring human being. He was quick to criticize areas of needed improvement, but he recognized and commended hard work, effort, and quality writing.

When the time came for choosing our final essay topics, I felt comfortable enough with Doug, and the class, to write my research paper on PMS. Mine was going to be a persuasive, expository essay with a bit of narrative. I knew that the paper would not only be read by Doug, but by several other class members as well, so I set out to do the best job possible. Also, the grade on this final project counted quite a bit, and, of course, that motivated me as well.

Not only did I go to the book store and buy every book that dealt with PMS, but I also called a friend of mine who was a research physician at a local hospital and asked her for any information that she could get her hands on. I ended up with more information that I ever thought possible. For days and days, I read through the books, the journals, and the articles. I was fascinated by the things that I was learning, and I was amazed at how much had been uncovered about PMS in just the last couple of years.

I became totally absorbed in the writing of my paper; in fact, I enjoyed every minute of it. Not only was I learning an incredible amount, finding things out that could possible help me, but I was writing what I felt to be my very best essay.

One of the books that I had purchased was about a woman who believed that through her research on, her knowledge about, and her own suffering from PMS, she had found a cure form PMS. Although I was quite skeptical at first, I found nothing harmful or dangerous in her approach. In fact, most of what she was recommending was very similar to what I was already doing. There were two major changes—one was to eliminate the progesterone injections.

I was so fearful of what might happen to me if I went off the progesterone. "Would I totally flip out?" I reminded myself that the progesterone hadn't helped me much over the past year anyway. I thought about it, prayed about it, and decided that I would give her program my undivided attention, even if that meant no progesterone.

The other major change in this program was the greatly increasing the amount of L-tryptophane (a natural over-the-counter amino acid which helped me to sleep better) from what I had been taking.[2] In fact, I had stopped taking it almost altogether. I had been relying on a glass of wine or two to help me to sleep. So, I began taking large doses of the L-tryptophane as were outlined and recommend in the book. As was also suggested, each day when I got home from work, I took a short nap—twenty to thirty minutes. Although this seemed impossible to do at time, I was determined to follow this plan to the "T".

Along with the L-tryptophane treatment, and the naps, I also carefully watched my diet. I had gotten incredibly sloppy and forgetful in this area. In fact, I was greatly disappointed in myself when I realized how much I had let myself slip away from the routine that Marcia had set up for me. I eliminated caffeine, chocolate, and sugar as much as I possible could. I concentrated on cooking the foods that were good for me, and started to learn to live without the things that were harmful.

I also tried to exercise a little. This was and still is my weakest area. But, at least a little was better than none! In addition to the exercise, I also began charting my physical and psychological symptoms again. I hadn't done this in months, and I found it extremely helpful. It served as a reminder to me, as well as to my family, when I had to be on guard for those difficult days.

As the days went by, I finished the work on my final essay, and I continued on with my new treatment plan faithfully. I turned my paper in to Doug, not knowing what the grade would be, and although that was still important to me, I felt I had gained so much more from writing the paper than a grade could ever reflect.

Oh, there he is! I'd better sit up and pay attention. Doug walks in and introduces himself to the class. Although he seems much more relaxed in this summer school session, I quickly realize that his expectations and requirements are just as stringent as ever. I know I've got my work cut out for me!

---

[2] L-tryptophane has since been found to be unsafe and should not be taken.

However, I'm glad to be here. Doug is a gifted teacher. I hope someday I'll get the chance to tell him that. I'd like also to tell him that he played a part in helping me to help myself. The past six months have been six of the best months of my life. However, it has taken a determined effort and full commitment on my part.

I have taken the L-tryptophane religiously. Everyday, when I come home, I lie down for about thirty minutes. This brief rest during the day, along with the deep sleeping at night, have done wonders in decreasing the anxiety, tension, and fatigue that have plagued me for so long. With a copy of "Foods to Eat/Foods to Avoid" stuck to my refrigerator, I have completely changed my eating and drinking habits. I can't believe how much better I feel since removing the large amounts of caffeine from my system. It hasn't been easy giving up Pepsi, regular coffee, and chocolate, but the absence of feeling nervous and irritable is certainly worth it. I have exercised a little, but I know I could use more.

Most importantly, because I have had the opportunity to feel like myself over longer periods of time, I have, once again, been able to practice my coping techniques. And because I feel better about myself, I have the self-confidence to go into battle on those dark days with a more optimistic attitude. More and more, I have begun to understand what a cyclical illness PMS is, and how crucial that understanding is towards getting well.

A woman who suffers severely from PMS has little or no self-esteem. Thus, she really has no desire to get better because she feels it is her fault or that she is the problem. Because she has no desire or very little will-power to get well, she then falls prey to the damaging psychological effects of the illness. Each month, as the woman feels more guilty and ashamed for her irrational behaviors, she internalizes that guilt and shame, blames herself, and her self-worth decreases again. The vicious cycle goes on and on—it can't be stopped without a long consistent period of time for healing, both physically and psychologically, to take place.

Because I have control of the PMS instead of the PMS having control me, I am able to continue to get better. I know there is still plenty of room for improvement and growth, but I feel as though I'm headed in the right direction. I also know that God will show me if I'm not...

As I leave class, I walk outside into the blistering sun. Walking to my car, I look up at the blue-white sky. The light is so bright that my eyes water just trying to catch a glimpse of the heavens. I have a word with our Master:

*God,*

*I know you're up there. It's so hot, but I know you're there! Thank you for making the pieces of the puzzle fit together so nicely—the emergency credential situation, the writing class with Doug, the paper on PMS, the books you had me read, the healing you brought to me. Now, I understand. I've go to trust you. You only want the best for me—only the best. Yes, I know. You are not through with me, yet. I've already accepted that fact—your work is never done. Oh, yeah, I do want to say one other thing—thanks for the A on the PMS final paper. I thought we deserved it!*

# Free And Faithful

It's our turn. Dan and I step forward to meet the receptionist at the desk. We show her our reservation confirmation slip, and she checks everything over. "Ok, you are all set. You will be in room number 473 on the Emerald Deck. Your luggage will be brought to your room for you. Enjoy your cruise." Dan and I excitedly move through the crowd and onto the gang-plank where we are greeted by two charming crew members. They stop us for just a moment to take our picture next to a large sign that says, "Azure Seas Cruises."

We walk quickly up the remainder of the plank and once again we are welcomed—this time by many crew staff. After the smiles and the handshakes (just like the "Loveboat"), we are directed to where our room is located. Dan and I hurry to our cabin, anxiously awaiting to see where we will be spending the next five days. Upon finding the room and opening the door, we discover a rather compact but charming room.

Everything is very clean and orderly. There is fresh fruit on the desk, ice and some cold drinks, and a note from our cabin steward. Again, we are welcomed by him and told that if there is anything that we need, just to call upon him.

Dan flops down on the bed with a tremendous sigh. I sit next to him and think about what a wonderful few days we are going to have. Dan hasn't had a vacation in three years, and this cruise looks like it will be the perfect opportunity to relax completely.

Before I know it, Dan's eyes are closed and he is sound asleep. I want to get our suitcases unpacked anyway, and there is no better time. As I begin opening the luggage and arranging all our belongings, I think about this past year and how faithful God has been.

Throughout the year, I continued on with the PMS program that I had been following. In spite of some additional stress (my step-son moving back in with us and my husband's very long hours at work), I have done remarkably well. The diet, the L-tryptophane, the afternoon naps and deep night's sleep, the coping techniques, the communication, the support from Alexis and Dan, and consistent prayer have all contributed to my well-being. Depression seemed to be the one area that plagued me the most, especially a few days right before my period, but other than that, the other symptoms had decreased greatly. I worked harder on getting better than I had anything else in my life, and just when I thought things were under control, I met another challenge.

About six months ago, an item in the news attracted my attention. Doctors had linked the deaths of several women with the amino acid L-tryptophane! Within just a few weeks, the FDA had pulled all L-tryptophane from the shelves, and it was virtually impossible to get!

I pressed the panic button. This was the one part of my program to which I had really attributed my vast improvement. How could this be happening? The one natural amino acid that I needed was killing people? It just didn't make any sense to me. Once again I started to ask myself and God "why?" Then, I stopped. This time, there was a strong resounding voice that said, "Trust Me," and I listened.

Even though I was discouraged, I trusted God. I kept on faithfully with the rest of my program. Dan checked with a health food store to see if there was anything else natural that I could take that would help me sleep. I tried a few herbs and vitamins, but they didn't help as much. I checked with my doctor who suggested a glass of warm milk before bed, eating some fresh turkey (it has L-tryptophane in it) and using a mild sedative. I chose to go with the milk before bed, which was a habit of mine anyway.

As the weeks wore on, I didn't sleep as well as I had wanted, but it also wasn't as bad as I had feared. I found that now I relied more on God than ever before. I prayed that He would help me to sleep, for Him to help me be less irritable, tense, and frustrated, and for Him to fill by body and mind with good positive feelings and thoughts. I came to the point where I knew I needed Him far more than I needed the L-tryptophane.

What's that noise? Someone is announcing something! I open our cabin door to listen more carefully. The captain is announcing that the ship will be leaving dock in ten minutes. I wake up Dan so that we can go on deck and wave good-bye to lots of people that we don't know. It will be fun though!

We make our way through the long hallways and up and down several flights of stairs. It is so easy to get turned around on a ship! Finally, we find where we need to be and nestle ourselves among the many people lined along the bow of the ship. The sun is shining brightly, a cool breeze is blowing slightly, the ocean is shimmering and shining, and carefree joyous people are madly waving their hands and arms at who knows who!?

Once we leave port, Dan and I make our way over to another deck where we can be alone. With our arms wrapped around one another, we stand for a long time—saying nothing, just enjoying the peace and solitude. There is something that I want to share with Dan, but it will wait until later.

After some time, we return to our cabin. We both feel exhausted from the previous hectic days. Dan has had to work incredibly hard in order to get this time off, and I have been traveling up in northern California visiting family and friends. One of the people that I really wanted to see and to talk with was Marcia—my friend and PMS physician. As I lie on my bed anticipating a wonderful nap, I think about the appointment I had with Marcia just five days ago.

As I drove up to the building where Marcia was now located, I couldn't help but think to myself what an incredible pioneer Marcia was. She believed in what she was doing, and she was willing to take the risks for that belief. When nobody else would treat PMS, let alone acknowledge that it existed, Marcia educated herself on PMS, believed her patients, and did everything she could to help them get better. Now, she has opened up her own PMS clinic in Stockton, and she continues to dedicate herself to the PMS cause.

After the expected hugs and smiles, Marcia and I sat down in her warm and cheery office. Here, she took a lengthy history (some of it repetitive from my previous treatment) and updated my chart from the three years since I had last seen her.

I explained to Marcia all that had happened in three years and how I was currently doing. She listened carefully and charted the information. When I was done, Marcia outlined a few things that she wanted me to do in addition to what I was already following.

The first thing was to begin a "three hour diet." What this meant was that I was to eat a small amount of complex carbohydrates every three or so hours throughout the waking day. She gave me some literature on the reasoning behind this. In very brief terms, it has to do with the importance of maintaining a steady blood sugar level throughout the day. The information explained in detail the relationship between the blood sugar level and adrenalin and how that relationship was an integral part of the PMS sufferer.

This new eating pattern seemed easy enough for me. In fact, I was looking forward to it. For years I had known that I was not able to go long periods of time without eating. If I did wait too long, I would get headaches, feel tense or irritable, and many times, my hands would shake. I never understood why.

The second thing that Marcia asked me to do was to begin taking a multi-vitamin, not just any vitamin, but one that had been carefully designed for the PMS woman. This particular vitamin would replenish the body with appropriate vitamins and minerals needed during the premenstruum and throughout the month, it would increase one's energy level, and it would help in overall healing of the body and the mind. I trusted her without question and began taking the vitamin immediately.

The third thing that Marcia reminded me of, was to exercise at least three times a week for at least fifteen minutes. As much as I wanted to find excuses, I knew there was none.

Marcia reminded me of the importance of the caffeine-free diet and the kinds of foods I should stress. I felt very good about my routine in that area—in fact, it was my strongest.

Lastly, we talked about ways to reduce stress and/or to deal with it. Again, I felt that I had made great strides in this part of my life. Sure, I still did worry a lot, but I was learning to give more and more over to God, and to give it over sooner than I had done in the past.

Before I left, Marcia reminded me to keep charting my symptoms (a new chart was provided that also allowed for vitamin intake and daily exercise) and to keep track of my diet on a food chart. By charting all this information, I felt that even more of a commitment was being made on my part towards feeling better. Perhaps, this was just a psychological mind-game; but nevertheless, it did make a positive difference.

When I walked out the door of the PMS clinic that day, I knew, without a doubt, that God had brought me here. I remember getting into my car, resting my arms on the steering wheel, laying my head on my arms, and talking to Him.

*Dear Lord,*

*Thank you for Marcia. Thank you for providing such a wonderful woman who is dedicated to helping women with PMS. Give her the strength to persevere, even when she comes up against stumbling blocks. Please bless her personally and professionally. Thank you also, Lord, for teaching me to not give up, especially when things don't seem to make any sense. Most importantly, thank you for showing me that when I trust you completely—when I give my life over to you totally—you are then free and faithful to do that good work in me. I know you are not done with me—I know you never will be—but I'm at peace with that too. I can't think of better Hands that I'd rather be in.*

There's that noise again! Good heavens. What

time is it? I stumble out of bed and open the cabin door. The captain is announcing that it is time for first seating at dinner. We've got ten minutes to get ready.

I wake up Dan, and we quickly shower and get dressed. After redoing my make-up and hair, we're out the door. We proceed to the dining room. After winding up and down the stairs several times and getting lost once or twice, we finally find it! We meet the people that we will be sharing our table with for the next five days, and we get to know our waiter and bus boy as well. Everyone is incredibly cordial, the service is flawless, and the food is exquisite. Dan and I look at each other and think the same thing, "Yes, this was the perfect vacation to take."

After dinner, Dan and I retreat to one of the upper decks for some fresh air and quiet time. It's cool and dark—but it's ever so peaceful. I have something on my mind I want to share with Dan and now seems the right time. "Dan, I would like to tell you about an idea that I have. I hope that you don't think it is silly." He reassures me that he won't, but still he has to nudge me on several times before I will say it. "Well, I was... thinking about writing a book ...during my vacation this summer. I thought I'd have the time to... write a book... What do you think?" I anxiously await his response, trying to hide my nervousness. As usual, he responds in his positive manner.

"I think that's a great! What is the book going to be about?"

I take a big breath and say quickly, "PMS—it's going to be about my struggle with PMS and how God helped me... do you think that's dumb?"

I desperately wait for his reassurance again and he calmly suggests, "Have you prayed about it? Have you talked to God?"

Somewhat frustrated (because I want an answer now!) I answer, "Well, no, I haven't....I guess I will...I...."

Dan gives me a big hug and laughs, "I really think you would do a fine job on such a book, but check in with HIM. He'll let you know soon enough if it's meant to be."

# Losing To Win

My stomach feels nervous inside, but it is a good kind of excitement. Dan and I enter through the large wooden doors and make our way through the crowd of teachers, administrators, board members, and other people who have chosen, for whatever reason, to attend this function—a reception for retiring teachers, for teachers who have served the school district in various capacities, and for teachers who have been chosen by their respective schools as 1991 Teacher of the Year. Dan and I locate the Jefferson group (the school where I teach), and nestle ourselves into the overly compacted area of chairs.

My principal and fellow teachers greet us warmly, and for the first time, the meaning of tonight begins to sink in. The staff at Jefferson Middle School has chosen me as Teacher of the Year, and I will be receiving an award for that honor. This means so much to me; it is hard to describe. I guess I really see it as another example of just how faithful God has been this past year.

"Good evening, everyone!" All heads turn towards the podium as the Mistress of Ceremonies greets the swarm of talkative educators, and many scurry back to their places as she continues to speak. My stomach feels another twinge of excitement, but then relaxes again as the Mistress informs us that before the acknowledgements for Teachers of the Year begin and the announcement of the winner of The Teacher of the Year for the district is made, she will first be honoring the retiring teachers. I lean back in my chair and take a big breath—it is going to be a while. As the Mistress begins calling out names, the clapping begins, the speeches proceed, and smiles and tears seem to fill the room. I smile too, not only for these dedicated teachers and the years of service they have given, but for this past year and what it has given to me.

When Dan and I arrived home from our cruise last summer, I continued on with the routine that Marcia had set up for me. The three hour diet, the vitamins, the exercise, the proper diet, and the charting procedures all became routine. Because I don't work in the summer, I must admit that the routine was easier to keep, and naturally, there was much less stress in my life. However, as the school year began, I was determined to maintain my program. I had to think of ways to assure myself that I would not slip. More and more, I began to realize, to accept, and to know that it was my responsibility to myself and to my family that I take care of my well-being.

When school started, I carefully planned out my days. In the morning, Dan would always lay out my vitamins on the table next to my breakfast. It was my job to fill the weekly pill container, but he made sure that I never forgot to take them. Also, in the morning, I had to remember to eat a complex carbohydrate within fifteen or so minutes after waking. I bought boxes of rye crisp and melba rounds—some for home and some for school. I actually put a small container in my medicine cabinet to hold a supply of rounds so that I could pop a couple into my mouth on my way into the shower! I have to admit that I do not always feel like eating at 5:00 A.M., but having the rounds or crisp right there made it convenient and eventually habit forming. I also took a couple of boxes to school and stored them in one of my desk drawers. Every morning at 10:00 A.M., I would reach inside and grab a couple for my mid-morning snack. This year, I was fortunate because I had my prep time (or free class period) in the early part of the day. However, if I hadn't, I still would have been able to grab a round or crisp in between class periods (with a five minute passing break). The point is, it doesn't take long to stuff something into one's mouth! I had lunch right at noon and when I left school at 2:30 P.M. or 3:00 P.M., I would again snack on a couple of rounds. I also kept some crackers in my car, in case I forgot or wanted a change of snack. This would hold me over until dinner with no problem, and then before bed, I would take the rest of my vitamins (which Dan brought to me) with a couple of shortbreads and a large glass of milk. This three hour eating pattern has become so vital to my feeling well that I rarely, if ever, forget my routine. If I do, it does not take long for a shaky or weak sensation to occur in my body (let alone a growling in my stomach) and I am quickly reminded to get a snack. One factor that concerned me about the three hour diet was the possibility of gaining weight. I remembered what Marcia had said, "It's not that you need to eat a lot, just often." Over the past year, I have gained two to three pounds and it has stabilized over the past six months. I am not even sure that it was the snacks themselves, but even if it was, the sanity has certainly been worth every pound!

Along with the three hour diet, of course, has been the constant implementation of the regular PMS diet. This too has continued to be an easy program to follow. When I grocery shop, I plan out the meals for the week, including sack lunches for both my daughter and myself. I still buy Dan and Alexis the goodies that they enjoy (chocolate ice-cream, Hershey Bars, caffeine drinks, etc.), but I also make sure that I have inviting substitutes like pink lemonade, freshly ground Irish-cream decaf coffee (a favorite of mine) and Pepperidge Farm Chessmen butter cookies to help me stay away from those other goodies. Every morning, along with my vitamins, Dan sets out a bowl of bran flakes with fresh fruit and a cup of decaf. Sometimes I eat a half piece of toasted French bread. For lunch, I take a sandwich (rye bread or wheat bread with tuna or fresh meats), a few potato chips, a hard boiled egg or fresh fruit, and a pickle. As a special treat, I might put in one or two Hershey kisses (but that is all!). For a drink, I make a large thermos of lemonade in the morning which lasts me all day. For dinner, I always cook a balanced meal, making sure to include a complex carbohydrate. I rarely, if ever, eat any kind of desert. If I did, I would avoid chocolate at all costs. I usually have milk with dinner, and then again before bed time. For some time, I have stayed away from any alcohol of any kind.

I am not saying or admitting that I never slip with the diet; however, if I do, I try to keep in mind where I am in my cycle (knowing when the more vulnerable days are) and doing whatever I can to balance out possible consequences. For example, if I go to the movies and have popcorn and a Pepsi, not only do I try to drink just a little of it, but if I start to feel irritable, I work especially hard at not showing it, I lie down for a few minutes if I can, and I eat very well for the rest of the day.

These routines may sound silly or even incredibly simplistic, but what one has to remember is that with PMS each part of the "get well" program must be followed consistently, especially for someone like me who can suffer severely. And, perhaps most importantly, when the day or days arrive when the PMS sufferer does not feel like taking the vitamins or eating the snacks (because of depression, or anxiety, etc.), the routine has already become so ingrained and such a way of life that it is less likely to be broken or to be ignored.

"Holli, you can stop clapping now. Everyone else is done." Oh, my goodness. I am a little embarrassed as Dan giggles and realizes that my mind was off somewhere else. Well, here we go, finally. The Mistress of Ceremonies is introducing someone who will announce the...what?..."the certificates for the teachers who have given of their time and energy to the district in various roles of service." As the names are called, my eyes focus on a teacher from our school who has an incredible energy level and who gives constantly to our school. I am thankful for her and people like her. At the same time, although I do not consider myself an energetic person, I am thankful for the strength that God has blessed me with this past year.

The strength that I am talking about is not only a physical strength, but an emotional one as well. Both strengths can be attributed to the other parts of the PMS program. Although exercising is still my weakest area in the program, I don't feel as though it has hurt my progress all that much. I am not trying to justify not exercising; instead, what I am saying is that for me, the lack of exercise does not seem to bother me as much as drinking lots of caffeine or eating mounds of chocolate. It is still important to exercise so as to relieve stress, and I do so when I can. However, in the free time that I have when I come home from school (which is about one half hour to forty -five minutes), I choose to spend that time taking a short nap. A twenty to thirty minute rest seems to strengthen me both physically and emotionally, especially during ovulation when I experience incredible fatigue. After taking a short nap, I feel like a new person—ready to prepare dinner, help with homework, and listen to the problems of the day that Dan or Alexis may have experienced. For me, just as the nap seems to diminish the tiredness, so too, the stresses of the day appear to break down and fall into perspective.

Another area of strength comes directly from learning to reduce stress in my life. Although voluminous books have been written on the topic of stress reduction, I feel that it is simply a choice that we make. If I want more stress in my life, I will say "yes" to more persons, places, and things. If I don't, I will say "no." Although I enjoy being active at school, at church, and at home with my family, I know that I will not be an enjoyable person to be around if I over-commit myself. Therefore, I limit my commitments, by saying "no" when I need to, and I reduce obligations even further during the more sensitive parts of the month. Along with reducing the stress in my life comes the strength not to feel guilty or bad that I have let others down or that I am not doing my part. Because I know that God knows my heart, and He knows me and what I am capable of, I can experience peace with the decisions that I make.

The last area of physical and emotional strength comes under the heading of communication. This communication takes all sorts of forms. The first form of communication manifests itself within the charting portion of the PMS program. By using the chart to designate menstrual problems and patterns, I am able to not only communicate to myself, but to my family as well - what, when, and how I need to do certain things. For example, as I am filling out the symptom chart and can identify that a more sensitive or difficult time of the month is approaching, I immediately pay closer attention to my diet, I make sure nap time is a priority, and I cut back on as many obligations as I can. Something that I have noticed this past year that has even added further to the importance of the menstrual charting is that my pattern in the PMS cycle has changed. In other words, instead of the depression, anxiety, tension, etc. all hitting at once from onset of ovulation and lasting up until the beginning of my menstrual period, I now experience symptoms of irritability, tension, and extreme fatigue during the first few days of ovulation, than all symptoms cease until the onset of the menstrual period when I suffer from slight to moderate depression for one day or two. If I hadn't used the charting procedure, I probably would not have been able to recognize the change in the pattern so quickly or have been able to deal with it so effectively. By knowing myself, my pattern, and by being able to anticipate changes, I have developed a physical and emotional strength and confidence that has greatly enhanced my well-being.

A second area of strength through communication has been through complete openness with Dan and Alexis: each sharing our feelings about PMS, how to communicate during PMS, or anything involving PMS. For example, as my daughter gets older (she is almost 12) and asks me about PMS itself or why I have said or done certain things in the past, I take the time to explain them to her. I can't take away the bad memories, but I can educate her as to why they took place. It is amazing how forgiving children can be when we let them in on our life experiences. One thing that I feel is extremely important is that when I am not feeling myself, I will usually tell Alexis so that both of us can make the necessary adjustments. As I have stated before, it is not an excuse for acting or behaving poorly; it is a preventative measure that ensures an understanding of the situation, and each of us makes allowances for one another. I smile inside as I think of one of the thoughtful gestures that Alexis does for me. When I tell her that I am going to lie down for a short nap, she knows why. She becomes almost motherly towards me. She comes into the bedroom to tuck me in and assures me she will watch the clock (as I have asked her to) so that I don't sleep too long. When my nap-time is over, she quietly comes into the bedroom, kisses me on the face, and gently tells me I have a few minutes to wake up. Although Alexis may need help with her homework or with her piano practicing, she unselfishly allows me this needed rest time.

As with Alexis, communication with Dan has been a source of strength as well. Our relationship continues to deepen and flourish because of our commitment that we have put towards effectively communicating. When Dan asks me if I am not feeling myself of if I am off key (our new code for PMSing), I do not feel threatened or upset at all. In fact, I am relieved that he feels free enough to ask. Dan does so many things that communicate his understanding and support of me, not only during PMS but on other days as well. Every morning, Dan writes me a note on my napkin and places it next to my breakfast. It is always a well-thought-out message that reveals his understanding of my feelings and emotions, and it is his way of expressing a positive thought for the day directly related to me. In additional to verbal discussions and written notes, Dan also communicates his care and concern in other unique and meaningful ways. When I am not feeling quite myself, it is not unusual for Dan to bring me flowers or to send them to me at the school. Often times, a simple note is attached that says, "I love you." Other times, Dan may put some money in an envelope and tell me to treat myself to something special (which could be anything from a new outfit, to a knickknack for the house, or to lunch with friends). On other occasions, no words or gifts or notes are exchanged, Dan shows his support through his actions – helping me with chores, helping me deal with people and/or situations, or most importantly, being there to hold and hug me.

These methods of communication may seem ridiculous or uncalled for to some women, but Dan and I have learned what works well for us. It may also seem as though I am a selfish and spoiled woman who expects her family to conform to her every mood. I am sure that my family will attest to the fact that the days where I need a little pampering are far and few now, and that for the most part, I am there for them - giving unselfishly in any way that I can. Don't get me wrong; I never say no to flowers or suggest Dan never sends me on a shopping spree. But, I know enough not to take it for granted!

The last area of strength comes from my communication with God. Although I have saved this for last, it certainly is not the least important; in fact, it is the most. I know that I would not have been able to maintain the progress I had made the last year nor would I have been able to improve upon that growth without God's help. When I pray at night, I ask God specifically to assist me with the PMS itself, with the PMS program, and to help me become a more giving wife, mother, friend, and person. I continue to pray—He continues to be faithful.

"Holli, hurry up. It is your turn!" Dan takes my wadded up Kleenex from my fingers and he smiles as I stand. As I walk towards the stage to pick up my plaque and shake the hand of one of the union officers, a feeling of great joy and accomplishment overwhelms me. My eyes fixate on the shiny gold and on the words "Teacher of the Year – Jefferson Middle School." The clapping echoes in my ears and I feel momentarily removed from this place. I close my eyes for a brief moment and give a quick thanks to the Master.

"That concludes our individual school awards, and now we will be announcing the district winners for Teacher of the Year, the Mistress of Ceremonies excitedly states. I sit erectly in my chair, nervously twisting another Kleenex while Dan gently holds my wrist. The Mistress explains that there will be three winners because our district is so large. She announces the first winner....I hold my breath....no, it isn't me. The second winner is....I twist my Kleenex so tightly that the end breaks off....no, not me. The third and final winner is....I take Dan's hand and feel the moisture in mine...but, no—it is not me. I take a big breath, smile, and begin clapping. yes, I am disappointed, but God knows my heart. I am truly grateful for what I have.

Dan gives me a hug as we stand to leave. After saying our goodbyes, we quickly sneak out a side door to beat the buzzing crowd. Dan has suggested a quiet dinner celebration for the two of us at our favorite restaurant. Without hesitation, I agree and before long we find ourselves face to face in a cool and serene atmosphere with familiar smells enticing our appetites.

As we click our ginger ale glasses, together, we celebrate the past year. Dan brings up a subject that we have discussed many times throughout the year, "How is your book coming along? Are you going to work on it some more this summer?" I assure him that I am; in fact, I can't wait to have the time to sit down at the word processor and continue working on it!

Later that night, after everyone is asleep, I lie in bed looking out my window at the stars. I can't sleep; I guess I am still wound up from the evening. Without realizing it I find myself talking to my Master.

*Thank you, Father, for everything but mostly for your faithfulness. I really wanted to win tonight, but I was ok with losing too. I trust you, and for whatever your reasons, winning was not meant to be. Once again, you have taught me something very valuable—that with losing, you can also win. With the PMS, when I lost everything—my self-esteem, my sanity, my family, my desire to live—you gave me the strength, the direction, and the will to go on, to fight, and to win. Yes, as I have said before, I also know that the battle is not over, and it may never be, but I'm on a winning* team! It is amazing when I think of how you work in our lives in so many different ways. If I had been well with the PMS four or five years ago, I don't believe that I would have had the courage to face the past head on and to share it with others, let alone write a book about it for other women who are feeling like I was. It is my deepest desire to help other women—to be on the giving end instead of the receiving one. I pray my book might be a vessel to reach hurting women, not only with PMS, but with other challenges as well. Lord, if it is meant to be, help me to find the words to make my book a good work—one that you would be proud of—one that you would call a winner.

# Piece Three

# The Joy Of Recovery

# Guidelines For Recovery

This section of the book is meant to give the reader some practical guidelines for PMS recovery. I have drawn upon the sources of some of the experts in the field of PMS. Please remember that there is no cure for PMS—it is a process of recovery. And, depending on the severity of the illness per individual as well as the uniqueness of each individual, the process may vary in form, length, and intensity.

## What Can A Woman Do About PMS?

I had the advantage of a friend giving me the name of physician who diagnosed and treated PMS. It is so important to locate a doctor who believes that PMS does exist and is willing to treat it correctly. There are many excellent PMS clinics throughout the country. Some of them are run by counselors, registered nurses, and physician assistants who are working with a medical doctor. These people have the time to work with PMS patients. When calling to inquire about a clinic or physician, ask them what their procedures are for diagnosing PMS. From all of the research that I have done, and from what I have learned from the experts in the field of PMS, it is my opinion that if the charting method is NOT used in the diagnosis of PMS, I would definitely go to a different place of treatment. Another obvious clue would be if you were told that treatment of PMS was with anti-depressants and/or diuretics. And, of course, if you were told that PMS didn't exist or that it was "all in your head," you certainly should go elsewhere. Most importantly, do not give up. There are doctors and other health care professionals out there who are ready and willing to help you. At the end of the appendix, I will include a phone number that may be able to assist you in locating PMS treatment in your area.

**How Will You Know If You Have Found The Most Effective Treatment Plan?**

As I have already stated, PMS symptoms manifest themselves in all kinds of forms (from the physical to the emotional), and in varying degrees. According to my research and personal experience, there are a number of guidelines that must be followed to insure the proper treatment of PMS. Of course, we should allow for some variation from clinic to clinic, and from doctor to doctor, but basically they should follow a program that includes:

◆ Diagnosis using the menstrual chart (3 month minimum)

◆ A diet plan - a list of foods to eat and foods to avoid

◆ The 3 hour diet - a complex carbohydrate every 3 hours of the waking day

◆ Vitamin supplement - one designed specifically for the PMS woman

◆ Stress reduction

◆ Exercise

◆ Rest

◆ Natural progesterone therapy - for severe PMS cases and with physician's recommendation.

◆ Counseling - needs will vary according to the woman and severity of PMS.

Let's take a look at each one of these items more carefully.

# Diagnosis Of PMS Using The Menstrual Chart

As I have already stated, different doctors use a variety of methods for diagnosing the illness; however, in the diagnosis of PMS, the use of the menstrual chart must be utilized. Physicians may also do a complete physical, including lab work, and they may take down a thorough medical history. The purpose of the menstrual chart is to determine if the physical and/or psychological symptoms associated with PMS are clustered around the menstrual cycle or if they are occurring haphazardly throughout the month. After two to three months of charting, one can easily recognize if there is a consistent pattern of symptoms or not. The kinds of menstrual chart will vary from clinic to clinic, but basically the chart will monitor two areas: the physical/psychological symptoms and the menstrual cycle. These charts are usually quite simple to fill out and do not take a lot of time. It is very important to fill them out accurately and thoroughly. Even when you may be feeling at your worst, record your symptoms as carefully as you can. Find a convenient place and time to post your chart so that you do not forget to fill it in. I keep my chart scotch-taped to the inside of my medicine cabinet. That way, as I am getting ready for bed that evening, I can accurately fill in the chart as to how I was feeling that day.

Even after your PMS is under control, I believe it is important to keep charting your symptoms. I have noticed over the years that my pattern of symptoms has changed. By knowing exactly when the trouble spots are, I can plan and prepare for those times.

On the following page is an example of a menstrual chart (Figure 1). As you can see, the PMS symptoms are clustered around the menstrual cycle in a consistent manner. Please note that both physical and psychological symptoms are charted. Also, remember that there is not just one PMS pattern (as discussed earlier in this appendix).

# FIGURE 1 - MENSTRUAL CHART

1st Day of menstrual flow is Day 1 of cycle.

Menses = M          Moderate = M          None = Leave Blank

Indicate Symptom severity: Severe = S

| Day of Cycle | 1 | 2 | 3 | 4 | 5 | 6 | 7 | 8 | 9 | 10 | 11 | 12 | 13 | 14 | 15 | 16 | 17 | 18 | 19 | 20 | 21 | 22 | 23 | 24 | 25 | 26 | 27 | 28 | 29 | 30 |
|---|---|---|---|---|---|---|---|---|---|---|---|---|---|---|---|---|---|---|---|---|---|---|---|---|---|---|---|---|---|---|
| Moodiness | M | | | | | | | | | | | | | S | S | S | M | M | M | M | M | M | M | S | S | S | S | S | | |
| Headaches | M | | | | | | | | | | | | | | | M | | | | | | | M | M | S | S | S | S | | |
| Anger | | | | | | | | | | | | | | M | M | M | | | M | M | M | M | S | S | S | S | S | S | | |
| Depression | S | | | | | | | | | | | | | | | | | | | | | | | | M | M | M | M | | |
| Menses | M | M | M | M | | | | | | | | | | | | | | | | | | | | | | | | | | |

Symptoms of PMS include both physical and psychological effects: Weight gain, bloating, irritability, food cravings, etc.
Jot down those which only apply to you.

Month 1          Date 10/14/92

Your physician or Clinician should ask for a minimum of three months charting for accurate diagnosis of PMS.

# A Diet Plan - A List Of Foods To Eat And Foods To Avoid

One of the most important items of an effective PMS treatment program is that of a dietary plan. Again, plans may vary from clinic to clinic, but there are some common strands that should be followed.

There are six kinds of items that should be avoided as much as possible.

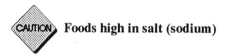 **Foods high in salt (sodium)**

These foods can worsen fluid retention; thus causing bloating and breast tenderness.

 **Sugar**

Sugar causes the blood sugar to fluctuate too much. It depletes the body's B-complex vitamins and minerals.

 **Alcohol**

Alcohol interferes with formation of glucose; thus prolonging low blood sugar and intensifying irritability, anxiety, headaches, and dizziness. It also disrupts the liver's ability to metabolize hormones, causing higher-than-normal estrogen.

 **Chocolate**

Chocolate increases craving for sugar and caffeine. It also causes breast tenderness and increases the demand for

B-complex vitamins.

 **Caffeine**

Caffeine causes fibrocystic breast disease and causes breast tenderness. Caffeine also depresses the appetite because of increased sugar in the blood stream. In addition, caffeine is a stimulant that causes nervousness, irritability, and shakiness.

 **Animal protein**

Animal protein (especially beef and poultry) has been injected with synthetic estrogens. Also, eating too much protein increases your body's need for some minerals.(Bender 151)

In addition to these, highly processed foods, fatty foods, and nicotine should also be avoided.

You might be asking yourself, "What is there left to eat?" Although they might not be your first choices, there are still plenty of healthful foods to eat.

Although I have always enjoyed the taste of salt, I have learned to do without it most of the time. I never cook with it, and have learned to substitute lemon juice or vinegar to flavor foods. Also, when shopping for foods, I keep an eye out for low sodium whenever possible.

Many women I have talked to have a great deal of difficulty in the area of sugar. Changing habits is not easy, but it can and will happen. First begin by cutting back on the amounts of sugar you are consuming, and then gradually taper off the number of occasions. If you are going to eat something sweet, try to it with a well-balanced meal.

Alcohol intake should be greatly reduced or eliminated. Research has shown that women who drink alcohol during their premenstrual phase have less of a tolerance level than during the remainder of their cycle. Non-alcoholic drinks or perhaps a light-wine would be preferable. Mineral water with a twist of lemon or lime also provides for a refreshing substitute.

Chocolate can also be tough to do without. Again, this is going to take will-power on your part. Do not set yourself up for failure. Begin a little at a time reducing the amount of chocolate intake. Then, gradually try to eliminate it as much as possible. Try to substitute fresh fruits instead, or perhaps even some carob. A friend of mine loves chocolate ice-cream. She eats a large bowl every evening. She also struggles with PMS. During a recent conversation, she told me she couldn't believe how much better she felt after eliminating her nightly treat!

Caffeine must be removed (or greatly reduced) from the diet. If you have been drinking large amounts of caffeine, it would be best to do this gradually. Remember, that caffeine is found not only in coffee and tea, but in chocolate, in drinks (colas, diet drinks, and other sodas), and in some non-prescriptive drugs. Check labels if you are in doubt. There are delicious decaffeinated coffees and teas on the market as well as natural juices. Also, there's no substitute quite like a cold glass of water.

Some of the best sources of protein can be found in fish, poultry, whole grains and legumes. Dairy products such as eggs, butter, cheese, milk, and yogurt should be limited, but not eliminated.

In summary, let's take a look at some of the foods to eat and some to avoid (Figure 2). Remember, you should consult your physician and/or nutritionist regarding the amounts of calorie intake that best suits you.

### FIGURE 2 - PMS DIET

| Foods To Eat | Foods to avoid |
|---|---|
| poultry | red meats |
| fish | dairy products (excess) |
| whole grains | candy |
| legumes | chocolate |
| dairy products (limit) | cake |
| fresh fruit | pie |
| green leafy vegetables | pastries |
| cereals (natural) | ice cream |
| safflower, sesame, and | coffee |
| sunflower oils | tea |
| seltzer | colas/sodas |
| mineral water | alcohol |
| tap water on ice | sugar |
| decaffeinated coffee/tea | fatty foods |
| | nicotine |

When I first started with my PMS diet, I did two things that really helped me that I hope will assist you. First, make a copy of the "Foods To Eat/Foods To Avoid" chart and put it on the refrigerator. When you go shopping, take the "Foods To Eat/Foods To Avoid" chart with you. Plan ahead and buy things that you need to have so that you don't find yourself running short and eating items that you should not have. Plan out your meals for the week so that you have well-balanced meals and so that you are not stuck eating fast food because you don't have anything at home to fix.

Next, make yourself an "Eating Chart" (Figure 3) and put it next to your other chart on the refrigerator. With your "Eating Chart," fill it in as you go along, or better yet, plan it out (either a day at a time or for several days). This way, you will be more accountable for what you are eating or have eaten. You will see it right there on the refrigerator and it will help you to stick to your PMS diet.

Another thing that I do is to keep my family's goodies separate from my snack foods. For example, their candy bars and cookies are in a different place in the pantry from my melba toast and rye crisps. There is no chance that they would want any of mine, but it helps me not to be tempted to eat their goodies if they are not right in my face!

Some of this PMS diet may seen very difficult for you or even impossible, but remember that as you begin to feel better and to notice a real difference in yourself, you will want to continue. Take it step by step, encourage yourself along the way, and don't be too hard on yourself for set-backs.

I've decided that even if I did not have PMS, I would still stick with this diet plan. It makes for better eating and therefore better health in the long run. It just seems to make good sense.

# FIGURE 3 - EATING CHART

| | SUN | MON | TUE | WED | THU | FRI | SAT |
|---|---|---|---|---|---|---|---|
| Early Morning Snack | 1 Rye Crisp | | | | | | |
| Breakfast | 1 egg<br>1 Piece Toast<br>Orange Juice<br>Decaf | | | | | | |
| Mid-Morning Snack | Fresh Fruit Apple | | | | | | |
| Lunch | Tuna Salad<br>Crackers<br>Decaf/<br>Ice Tea | | | | | | |
| Afternoon Snack | 2 Graham Crackers | | | | | | |
| Dinner | Chicken<br>Baked Potato<br>Green Beans<br>Decaf/<br>Ice Tea | | | | | | |
| Bedtime Snack | Triscuits<br>Herbal Tea | | | | | | |

# The 3 Hour Diet

The 3 hour diet, often referred to as "the 3 hour starchy diet" is an integral part of the PMS treatment program. Before taking a look at how to implement the 3 hour starchy diet, let's take a look at why it is important to the PMS woman.

In very simple terms, the goal of the 3 hour diet is to maintain a steady blood sugar level throughout the day. When the blood sugar level drops, there is a spurt of adrenalin (which takes sugar from the cells in order to raise the blood sugar level). It is the hormone adrenalin which is responsible for the feelings of panic, irritability, depression, and which causes a woman to behave in a violent and an irrational manner. Eating a small amount of a complex carbohydrate will cause a gradual rise in blood sugar level with a gradual drop when the blood sugar level falls. If you eat sugar, you will experience a rapid rise in the blood sugar level as well as an abrupt fall.

The 3 hour starchy diet is simple to implement. In fact, it has been my experience that because I have felt so much better when sticking with the diet, I rarely, if ever, forget to follow it. Every three hours during the waking day, you should eat a small amount of complex carbohydrate. This means eating something starchy within fifteen minutes of waking, again at breakfast, again at mid-morning, at lunchtime, at mid-afternoon, at dinner and again at bed-time. Remember, you do not have to eat a lot—just a small amount each time. If you are doing this correctly, you will notice very little weight gain, if any. In fact, you might find that you eat even less at meal time because you are not so ravenous.

What kinds of food should you eat? There is a variety from which to choose: whole grains, nuts, breads, pastas, rice, potatoes, biscuits, crisps, crackers, crispbreads, popcorn, and many others. Remember, however, to watch the salt (sodium) levels. Another point to bring out here is that each of these foods is low in calories when eaten just as they are. It is when rich sauces are added to pastas, gravies are poured onto mashed potatoes, and chocolate is blended with cookies that calorie intake could become a concern.

As you will do with your regular diet, plan ahead for your snack food! Buy several different kinds of crackers, crisps, and biscuits to have on hand. Also mark your snacks down on your eating chart to keep yourself on target. Arrange to have the snacks in convenient places for easy access. Keep a tray of crisps in your medicine cabinet or bathroom drawer for early morning. Keep some biscuits or cookies in the night stand next to your bed for evening. If you are working outside the home, or if you spend quite a bit of time in your car taking children to and fro, keep some graham crackers in the glove compartment or by the drivers seat for easy reach. Be sure to keep a supply of breads or toasts at your place of employment, and always keep a few crackers in your purse. You never know how long you might be kept waiting someplace!

It is important to not only implement the 3 hour starchy diet during the premenstruum, but also throughout the entire month. Something that I remember Dr. Dalton sharing at a PMS Symposium was that if a woman deviates from the three hour intervals of eating for just one time, it can alter her body chemistry for up to a week. In other works, we can't go around eating anything we want at anytime we want for several days or even a couple of weeks, then, abruptly change our eating habits and expect it have immediate, if any, results. This is especially significant for women with PMS because we need to think ahead, plan ahead, and stick with it in order to experience recover.

# Vitamin Supplement

Although there is some disagreement among the experts as to the need for a vitamin supplement, I have experienced that it too has been an important part of the PMS treatment program. You should discuss this with your physician and/or nutritionist and make a decision that is suitable for your dietary needs. At the end of the appendix, I will give you the name and phone number of an excellent pharmacy that specializes in vitamins for PMS and who is qualified to answer your specific questions.

In Stephanie DeGraff Bender's book entitled *PMS: A Positive Program to Gain Control,* she includes a vitamin and mineral chart that is very helpful in explaining the functions of vitamin supplementation. (147-148) (Figure 4).

# FIGURE 4 - VITAMIN AND MINERAL CHART

| Vitamin | Suggested Daily Supplement | Function |
|---|---|---|
| A | 15,000 I.U. | Alleviates premenstrual acne and oily skin. |
| B Complex, (riboflavin, niacin, thiamin) | 50mg to 100mg | Prevents loss of the B vitamins caused by emotional stress, which results in irritability and fatigue. |
| B6 | Doses from 50mg to 200mg | Minimizes many premenstrual symptoms such as food cravings, fluid retention irritability, breast tenderness, fatigue and mood swings. Has been linked to release of the brain's neurotransmitters, dopamine and serotonin, which elevate mood. Plays a part in the metabolism of carbohydrates and proteins and can reduce food cravings when taken premenstrually. |
| E I.U. | 300I.U. to | Helps to reduce fibrocystic disease 600 (benign lumps in the breasts). |
| Calcium | 150mg | Helps prevent menstrual cramps. |
| Magnesium | 300mg | Helps prevent menstrual cramps, helps control sugar cravings. |
| Zinc | 25mg | Helps control acne. |
| C | 250mg to 1000 mg | Helps control stress and premenstrual allergies. |
| D | 100 I.U. | Helps control premenstrual acne. (should not be taken in large doses) |

From the research that I have done, it has also been suggested that vitamin B6 not be taken by itself for PMS. Instead, the entire B complex should be taken together. Again, please consult with your physician of nutritionist before taking any over-the-counter vitamins or non-prescription vitamins.

If vitamins are going to be a part of your treatment program, put them in a place that is easily accessible and where you won't forget to take them. I recommend putting them in a daily pill container. Fill it with the week's vitamins and make it a routine to take your pills at around the same time every day. This way, it will simply become part of your daily plan; in fact, it will become second nature to you.

# Stress Reduction

We all experience stress in our lives. It is a simple fact, but one in which the PMS woman must be especially concerned.

During the free PMS period of our cycle, we probably deal with stress very much the way most people do. We are irritated, frustrated, or fatigued, but we manage to keep our emotions under control. Unfortunately, when we enter into our PMS phase, we often respond irrationally and illogically to the same stresses that we were able to manage just days before. Situations, pressures, and problems are exacerbated to the point that we feel overcome by the stresses put upon us. Therefore, not only do women with PMS need to learn to manage the stress that they cannot avoid, but more importantly, they must plan ahead to reduce the stress in their daily lives.

As far as managing the stresses that cannot be avoided, each woman needs to incorporate those methods into her routine which seem to work best for her. Many books have been written on relaxation techniques involving breathing and muscle exercises. If this is what you enjoy doing and find it works for you, then it would be best to continue such a program.

Exercise (which will be discussed in more depth later) can help alleviate stress. Exerting yourself physically provides an excellent opportunity to release pent-up tension and anxiety. If you are already following an exercise program, I encourage you to continue—especially during your PMS phase. Until recently, I rarely, if ever, exercised. Then, several months ago, I began jogging every morning for at least twenty to thirty minutes. I was amazed at how much tension seemed to actually drain from my body and mind as I was jogging. I have also noticed a marked improvement in the amount of stress that I feel during my daily routine and in the manner in which I deal with that stress. If you do not exercise, I encourage you to find something you enjoy doing and to begin implementing a regular routine.

Rest (which will be discussed further) is also an important ingredient in the recipe for stress reduction. It is only common sense to realize that for most of us, we do not handle stress well when we are tired. As I shared in my story, taking naps is an essential element of my recovery process. Remember, naps need not be long—fifteen to twenty minutes will suffice. It's incredible how refreshed you will feel after a short nap and how stress of the day will seen to melt away. If you have small children or other obligations that keep you from a short nap, try sitting down in a comfortable chair, propping your feet up, and drinking a refreshing drink (no caffeine!). Making dinner or folding clothes can wait for twenty minutes while you give yourself a breather. This little break can do wonders for your peace of mind.

Another daily stress reducer is spending time meditating on God's Word and/or praying. Sometimes we allow our minds to play little tricks on us by saying, "Oh, I wish I had time to read a verse and meditate on it, but I've got so much to do...I just don't have time." There are many clever ways in which we can make the time to spend a quiet moment with our Master. Keep your Bible readily available. Before you jump into the shower or begin making breakfast, read a verse or two. Then while you go about your routine, practice memorizing the verse and think about its meaning. A friend of mine keeps her Bible right on her bathroom counter. While she is putting on her make-up and fixing her hair, she manages to read at least a chapter or two. If you jog, run, or do your exercising alone, spend time with the Lord! What a perfect opportunity to communicate with Him! Also, there are many wonderful devotionals out on the market that contain brief but meaningful daily messages. Next to my kitchen sink, I keep a daily calendar that has a Bible verse and its application printed on it for each day (somewhat like a daily devotional but more brief). It never ceases to amaze me how appropriate each verse is for that given day!

In addition, my husband and I pray together each morning before we leave for work. We find, and perhaps you will too, that it never hurts to have a little extra armor as we go out to battle the stresses of the day. Take advantage of those often too few but free moments of your day. Grab hold of them, spend a moment in prayer or meditation, and then relish in the splendor of support that you will feel throughout your daily routine.

Last, but certainly not least, is planning ahead to reduce stress. For the PMS woman, this is vitally important. One of the best ways

I have found is to plan out my weekly (and monthly) calendar. Whether you are married with children, a single parent, or a single woman, I urge you to do this. choose a day (perhaps a quiet Sunday afternoon) to sit down (with husband and children if possible) and to plan out your week. What meetings, activities, appointments, or obligations do you have? Write these down on your calendar. Have you overloaded your week? If so, what can you change or eliminate? Who can help out? Who can compromise? At the same time you are doing this, take a look at your PMS chart. Where are you in your cycle? Is this week a good one or are you entering into a sensitive time? Remember, it is your choice to say no to overloading your schedule. Also, while you are planning your weekly schedule, take a look at the weekend planning for the month. Do you want to have friends over for dinner, to get away for a weekend, to have relatives visit, or to enjoy a restful obligation-free weekend at home? Plan this out with your family members now—again keeping your PMS chart in mind. Coordinate the more stressful activities during your free PMS period and allow for more relaxation and calming events during your PMS time.

While being a great stress reducer, this calendar planning is really an invaluable communication tool for you and your family. It's a positive way for all of you to support one another while being sensitive to the needs of everyone. I take the calendar routine one step further. I keep a small calendar in my purse (like a day-runner) where I record all the information I keep on the family calendar. This way, as I encounter additional requests, appointments, and obligations during the week, I can quickly refer to my personal calendar to judge whether I am overdoing it or not. Yes, it is difficult to say no to other people, but women with PMS need to understand that there are times where we must say no and not feel guilty about it. Our health and our relationships are more important than our duties. Neither ourselves nor our loved ones need suffer if we are realistic in our commitments.

Once again, PMS clinics and doctors may vary in their approaches to stress reduction. Find what is comfortable for you and make it a routine part of your recovery process.

# Exercise

Exercising is one of the most important aspects of the PMS recovery program. I admit that I didn't realize this until recently, but I strongly advocate a routine of exercise for all women (PMS or not). As I stated earlier, when exercising, pent-up tension and anxiety are released. Exercising just makes you feel good, both physically as well as emotionally. In my research, I discovered that as a result of exercising, your brain produces endorphins that naturally relieve pain and also elevate your mood (Bender 154). In addition to the physical and emotional benefits, exercise gives you a mental boost because you know that you are doing something good for yourself. As with the other aspects of the PMS program, exercising is an important preventative measure.

If you have not been in a regular exercise program, set yourself up for success, not failure. Start slowly and build up a little at a time. Choose a type of exercise that you enjoy and that is readily available to you and convenient for you. If you have small children, it may be impossible to go to the gym three times a week, but there are excellent fun work-out videos that you can do right in your living room. Jogging, running, cycling, and swimming are exercises that can be done early in the morning (before the children wake up) and that are very inexpensive! As I suggested, start with realistic goals. I remember the first morning that I decided that I was going to start jogging. I was going to do a mile run even if it killed (and it almost did!). Your body is usually the best judge of what your limits are. Start at a comfortable level, increase your distance, time, etc. as you feel fit, and pat yourself on the back even as you make small strides.

According to the research, the recommended amount of exercise is a minimum of three times a week for at least twenty to thirty minutes. Be sure to check with your doctor if you have any concerns or medical problems that may need special attention with regards to your plan of exercise. To insure the successful implementation of a regular exercise routine, set a time during the day that works best for you (and your family). Stick with the designated time as much as possible. That way, it will naturally become a part of your PMS program along with the other aspects.

# Rest

The sleep needs of women obviously vary greatly from woman to woman. You know yourself best in this area. Are you getting enough sleep? Are you getting deep restful sleep? Are you receiving uninterrupted sleep? Do you feel less than yourself if you do not get the kind and amount of sleep that you desire? All of these questions are important. You must be honest with yourself in answering these questions and in deciding whether rest is an issue with you or not.

A friend of mine has four small children, works outside the home, keeps an immaculate home, and is a loving and giving wife and mother. She functions on an average of five (or less) hours of sleep a night. Although she has jokingly shared with me that she has her PMS moments, she doesn't feel that her sleep patterns affect her to any significant degree. On the other hand, one of my sisters requires a minimum of eight hours of sleep a night. Both she and I know what our bodies need and therefore, we make sleep a priority in our routines. Yes, it is easier because both she and I do not have young children. However, if sleep is an important part of feeling better for you, you need to communicate that to your family members and to make the necessary adjustments. Perhaps there are times during the day when you can nap with your young children. Ask your husband to put the children to bed for you a few times a week so that you may climb into bed early to get that much needed extra rest. Again, be sensitive to your PMS chart. You may need a little extra rest just during your premenstruum and even just for a day or two. When do you feel the most fatigued? Be aware of those times, communicate them to your loved ones, and together adjust your schedules accordingly.

Along with getting enough sleep is the issue of quality sleep. It is not uncommon for women suffering from PMS to have difficulty sleeping in a deep restless manner (especially during the premenstruum). This is why exercise and stress reduction are so vital. They both help alleviate tensions that often interfere with quality sleep. There are other suggestions that may help out a little: drinking a glass of milk at bedtime, eating your nighttime starchy diet snack right before you go to bed, and keeping some starchy snack readily available in case of nightly awakenings. A physician friend of mine recently reminded me of the importance of maintaining the blood sugar level (even late at night) to help minimize those restless surges. Herbal teas have also be recommended to me, but I haven't met with much success. Check with your nutritionist for other natural approaches or suggestions.

Once again, if sleep is important to your well-being, begin by making the necessary changes. As with the other aspects of the recovery process, you can only benefit by taking care of your needs.

# Natural Progesterone Therapy

Natural progesterone therapy is one aspect of the PMS recovery program that may not be necessary for all women (probably not those suffering from mild to moderate symptoms). However, it is indeed of extreme importance to the woman who does not feel relief from her PMS symptoms after she has implemented that other self-help aspects of the recovery program. According to the experts in the field of PMS, a woman and her physician (or clinician's recommendation with a physician) should determine if there is due cause for implementation of progesterone therapy. If a woman is suffering severely from PMS—that is—her symptoms are interfering significantly with her personal and professional life, she may be a candidate for natural progesterone therapy (Bender 156). As I told in my story, my symptoms were so severe that they were damaging to my relationships as well as to my sense of being. I needed help in stabilizing my emotions so that I could begin to rebuild my life. For myself, as with many other women, the self-help aspects were certainly a beginning, but the natural progesterone therapy provided me with the relief that I so desperately needed.

You may be wondering what is progesterone therapy? According to Stephanie Bender (156):

> Progesterone therapy is supplementation of the body's supply of progesterone. Progesterone is one of the two principal female hormones, and the body produces it during the second half of the menstrual cycle (starting at ovulation) as well as during pregnancy. One of the most commonly held theories about the origin of PMS is that a woman suffers from PMS because her body does not produce sufficient levels of progesterone during the premenstrual phase of her cycle. The purpose of progesterone is to raise the body's progesterone level during that time.

It is important to note that natural progesterone is not a cure for PMS. However, when it is administered properly, along with the other aspects of the PMS program, the severe symptoms can be eliminated or sharply reduced (Norris 243).

It is also important to note that according to Dr. Dalton (184), there are no contraindications for the use of progesterone and there are no risks of progesterone causing cancer. In fact, Dr. Dalton states that progesterone is used in the treatment of some cancers. In addition, Dr. Ronald Norris confirms that the side-effects of progesterone are uncommon and not very serious (251):

1. Shortening of the menstrual cycle.
2. Lengthening of the menstrual cycle.
3. Spotting at mid-cycle.
4. Spotting in the premenstruum.
5. Erratic cycles.
6. Hives or rash.

Each of these minor problems can be addressed by making adjustments in the timing of progesterone treatment or in the methods of administration. The most commonly used methods of administering progesterone therapy are through the use of suppositories, through liquid rectal suspension, and through intramuscular injections.

One serious note of caution needs to be mentioned at this point. Progesterone is a natural substance. Synthetic progesterone is called progestogen or progestin. Synthetic progesterone is of NO value in treating PMS. Chemically it does not duplicate natural progesterone. This is important because physicians often erroneously prescribe progestogens (oral medications) for the treatment of PMS (Bender 159). One such commonly prescribed drug is called provera—a synthetic progestogen. Dr. Ronald Norris states that it is vitally important to differentiate between natural progesterone and synthetic progestogen because many progestogens have properties that antagonize and worsen premenstrual syndrome (245).

If you and your physician are considering natural progesterone therapy, I urge you to call the PMS Access toll-free number listed at the end of the book. Madison Pharmacy Associates welcomes your questions and will provide you with accurate professional advice.

Although I am not currently taking natural progesterone, if I felt the need, I certainly would not hesitate to begin taking it again. Some women have expressed to me that they feel embarrassed or ashamed because they cannot handle their PMS by themselves. They view the taking of progesterone therapy as a sort of weakness or crutch. I try to comfort them by reminding them that **PMS is an medical illness**—in fact—it is multi-faceted illness that requires a great deal of will-power on all of our parts to keep it under control. If we require medication to assist us in maintaining our balance so that we can strengthen our will-power, then we need to put our egos aside and begin therapy. Please remember, you are not alone in how you feel and think...we are in this together.

## Counseling/Support Groups

Counseling, as with progesterone therapy, is an area that may not affect all women with PMS. This is a very individual and somewhat private aspect of PMS recovery. A woman must be willing to honestly assess her level of PMS and determine whether it has altered how she perceives herself as a person. She must also be open as to whether the PMS has affected, changed, or even harmed other family members (or loved ones) and her relationships with them. Women who suffer severely with PMS, as I did, should not be afraid of counseling. Sometimes there is much hurt that has been inflicted upon those closest to us, and we and they need the time, the opportunity, and the direction that a professional counselor can provide to address those hurts and to begin the healing process.

Even after the PMS is under control, it is important to remember two things. First of all, YOU may be feeling better than you ever have before and therefore you are ready and willing to embark upon your new found life. However, family members or loved ones may still be carrying around unseen wounds that need attention. It is my belief that only through well-directed communication can those wounds be effectively addressed. Remember how I shared in my story that I was surprised at how much my husband had been hurt by my PMS. I don't think I would have realized that as early on as I did had it not been from our counseling sessions together.

Secondly, if you have suffered severely and chronically from PMS, there are a couple of other factors to keep in mind. Chances are that your self-esteem and self-worth are quite low. Working through those selfless feelings takes a lot of time and communication. Most importantly, I believe it takes a professional who can guide you positively and in a direction that brings growth and strength. To expect that you can do this entirely by yourself is unrealistic, and to expect family members or loved ones to provide this for you is unfair. Another vital and critical factor to keep in mind (if you have suffered severely and chronically) is that because the PMS is under control, the negative behaviors that have accompanied you for so long might not just go away automatically. As I shared in my story, even after I was feeling great physically, it was still very difficult to keep from reverting back to the negative behaviors. Changing attitudes, habits, and behaviors is extremely difficult, but it is often necessary. I encourage you to let the professionals assist you with behavior modification techniques. There is nothing more peaceful than experiencing the unleashing of negative behaviors that bind and restrict us and to be given the opportunity to grab hold of new and more productive ways of living.

When looking for a counselor, you need to keep in mind the same guidelines as when looking for a physician. Obviously you want one who is sympathetic to PMS. Many PMS clinics have professional counselors on staff, and if not, they may be able to recommend one to you. Also, see if there is a PMS support group in your area. Chances are that a recommendation could be made from such a group.

Many women do not need professional counseling, but they do find great encouragement and identification within a PMS support group. These groups may/may not be led by professional counselors, but they should have a common goal of bringing women together for the purpose of supporting one another. Not too long ago, a young mother called me who has suffered from PMS since she was eighteen. She asked me if there was a support group in her area (which there was not). She talked about the need to know that there were other women who felt and experienced the same kinds of emotions and situations she went through. She expressed feelings of isolation and lack of support in her family.

A support group can provide wonderful validation for a PMS woman as well as a release valve for frustrations. Many times, just knowing that you are not alone in what you feel can be the seed that roots the process of healing.

The PMS Access number at the end of the book can refer you to support groups in your area. If you do not have one, perhaps you can be instrumental in getting one started. An excellent place to start a support group would be in your own church! Remember, part of getting well is the willingness to reach out to others and to begin putting the pieces of the PMS puzzle in their place.

# How Can I Do All Of This?

You might be asking yourself, "How can I do all of this?" You can and you will. After you have consulted with a PMS physician and/or clinician, or even if you feel like instituting some of aspects of the recovery program by yourself, be careful not to set yourself up for failure. Begin a little at a time, implementing each phase of the program as it best suits you. It may be helpful to make yourself a chart (see Figure 5) and add to it as you feel comfortable and have the time. I would recommend starting out with the three hour starchy diet and the PMS diet. Many women who suffer mildly to moderately often experience a significant loss of symptoms by implementing the three hour starchy diet. Stick with the diets for two or three weeks, then add your exercise, then work on stress reduction, and so on. As you add each item to your routine, mark it on your chart so that you will hold yourself accountable. Please keep in mind what was discussed about progesterone therapy. Self-help techniques may not be enough to bring the PMS under control, and I urge you to take advantage of the medication available to you through your physician.

Place your recovery program chart on the refrigerator or put it in a place that is convenient for you to fill out at the end of each day. At the end of a month or a designated time period, reward yourself for your accomplishments. At the same time, do not be too hard on yourself for your setbacks.

As you look over your chart, doesn't it make good sense to be doing these things? Even if you or I did not have PMS—the diets, vitamins, exercise, rest, stress reduction—would all make for a healthier lifestyle. It feels good to be the winning side rather than the defeated one.

# FIGURE 5 - RECOVERY PROGRAM CHART

Successfully Completed = +

Partially Completed = ✓

Try Again or Not Applicable = -

| Month: Dec. | 1 | 2 | 3 | 4 | 5 | 6 | 7 | 8 | 9 | 10 | 11 | 12 | 13 | 14 | 15 | 16 | 17 | 18 | 19 | 20 | 21 | 22 | 23 | 24 | 25 | 26 | 27 | 28 | 29 | 30 | 31 |
|---|---|---|---|---|---|---|---|---|---|---|---|---|---|---|---|---|---|---|---|---|---|---|---|---|---|---|---|---|---|---|---|
| Charting Symptoms | | | | | | | | | | | | | | | | | | | | | | | | | | | | | | | |
| PMS Diet | | | | | | | | | | | | | | | | | | | | | | | | | | | | | | | |
| 3 Hour Diet | | | | | | | | | | | | | | | | | | | | | | | | | | | | | | | |
| Vitamins | | | | | | | | | | | | | | | | | | | | | | | | | | | | | | | |
| Rest | | | | | | | | | | | | | | | | | | | | | | | | | | | | | | | |
| Exercise | | | | | | | | | | | | | | | | | | | | | | | | | | | | | | | |
| Stress Reduction | | | | | | | | | | | | | | | | | | | | | | | | | | | | | | | |

Reward yourself at the end of the week and at the end of the month!

# Piece Four

# How Our PMS Affects Those We Love

# A Message To The Children
# Of PMS Sufferers

*Life is not easy for children growing up today. It is even more difficult if Mom is suffering from PMS. I asked my daughter if she would mind sharing some of her insights and feelings involving her experiences with PMS. She heartily agreed. Perhaps you can relate to what she has to say. I hope that you might find comfort in the fact that you too are not alone in what you are going through.*

---

My name is Alexis and I am almost 12. I will be going into seventh grade. My mom has had PMS for about as long as I can remember. It's been since I was about five or six—for about the past seven years. I've learned a lot about PMS, about what happens to my mom, and to me, and what both of us can do to help it go away.

When I think about what PMS is, I describe it in this way. It is something that happens every month. I am never sure when in the month, but I know it will happen. When my mom gets it, she will usually be mad, sad, tired, or really frustrated.

The one thing that I dislike so much about my mom's PMS is that she gets so angry that it makes me feel really sorry for her. And sometimes, I even feel afraid. I just want to go right up to her and take all this frustration and anger and throw it all away - but I can't. Another thing that I don't like about my mom's PMS is that if she is having it on a day where I am really sad or depressed, I can't show it or get any comfort from her because she is too emotionally caught up with herself.

I've learned to do a couple of things for myself when my mom is having PMS. The best thing for me is to keep to myself. I stay in my room more—I try to stay out of the way. I have found that this is a safe thing to do. It helps to avoid any misunderstandings or arguments, especially over little things that we normally would not argue about.

I've also learned to do things for my mom when she is having PMS. For example, I might offer to do some ironing for her or perhaps some vacuuming. Just the fact that I am willing to volunteer my help (without being asked) seems to make her feel better. I have also learned that I should not talk back if my mom asks me to do something. One important thing I do for my mom is to encourage her. One way I do that is by suggesting to her that she take a short nap if she is not feeling like herself. I say it kindly and sincerely because I know how much better she will feel afterwards, and I know she will be very giving to me when she is rested. I also encourage her through my words and actions. For example, if my mom has had a bad day with PMS, we usually talk about. She is quick to say she is sorry and to ask for my forgiveness. I am quick to forgive her and give her a big hug.

The most important thing I've learned about PMS is that there is help available. My mom tells me that there is no cure, but when I see how much she has changed over the past couple of years, I know that she is getting better all the time.

I started seeing changes in my mom after she went to see a PMS doctor. Now, she controls her emotions a lot better. For example, she used to get so angry and yell a lot. Now she is much more calm. Also, I used to be kind of afraid—not knowing when my mom was going to explode or how bad it was going to be. I don't worry about that anymore - my mom's behavior is stable. Overall, she seems to be a much happier person.

These changes make me feel a lot better. Our family is happy and normal. One thing that is wonderful is that I know that my mom can take better care of herself without me helping as much. What I mean is that I watch her do all these things in her PMS program which have made her so much better and so, I hardly have to do anything!

If you think your mom has PMS, please do not be discouraged. There are several things you could do. First, I would read some books about it in your spare time and tell your mom what you think she has. I would suggest to her that she go to see a PMS doctor. Help your mom out with chores and just be really loving to her. Once your family understands what you mom has, talk about it and learn more about it. Always encourage your mom to not eat too many bad kinds of food such as Pepsi, chocolate, and other things that have a lot of caffeine and sugar in them. One thing that I do for my mom that helps her (and me) a lot with her PMS is that I pray and ask God to help her and guide her through the day.

Also, remember that you are not alone in how you feel. There are many, many children out there who share the same fears, hopes, and dreams. We want our moms to feel better, not only for themselves, but for us too. There's nothing wrong with wanting that.

# A Message To The Men
# In The Lives Of PMS Sufferers

*It is my belief that the men in the lives of PMS sufferers (whether they be husbands, boyfriends, or close friends) are the other victims of the illness. The abuse that you men receive during a PMS episode can in no way be justified. Perhaps you can find comfort, understanding, and even answers from what my husband, Dan, has to share.*

Gentlemen, it is not always easy for us to open up and talk about such private matters, but with PMS being the kind of illness that it is (one in which there are multiple victims), I feel that it is mandatory that I do so. I will be very candid as I share with you my feelings, insights, frustrations, and yes, even solutions. Be confident, as I share my side of the PMS story, that you are not alone..nor are you without answers.

Let me begin by first describing to you what Holli's PMS was like before she sought help. When I first started dating Holli, she revealed to me only the Holli that she wanted me to see or to become acquainted with at the time. It was not until several months had elapsed that I was permitted to get a first-hand glimpse of the stranger that lurked within Holli, and even then I did not know what or who I was encountering. All I knew was that occasionally, and for no apparent reason, Holli, the woman I had fallen in love with, would be transformed into an irrational and out of control stranger.

The stranger usually would manifest herself through horrendous fits of anger and rage—swinging fists and shouting obscenities. More often than not, the violent fits were followed by a radical mood swing, resulting in a deep and prolonged state of depression and remorse.

When initially confronted by this other Holli, I was scared to death. I was frightened because I felt I was responsible for the change(s) in her, and I was concerned that our relationship was at risk.

As time passed I learned to resent and dislike the stranger and her disgusting appearance and behaviors. Consequently, I chose to retaliate, aggressively engaging my foe whenever possible—even if it meant losing the person I loved.

Thankfully, I was struck by a bolt of empathy and the desire to know and understand why these uncharacteristic outbreaks were occurring. Innately, I was convinced that there must be a logical/biological explanation for what was taking place. It was during my search for an answer that our mutual friend, Pat, introduced me to the stranger's suspected name—PMS!

Not only did the PMS affect me, but it certainly had a great impact on my relationship with Holli as well. The first six months of our relationship was similar to a honeymoon. The time we spent together was filled with laughter and romance, and somehow Holli was able to prevent exposing the stranger within. This was an intensely blissful period in our courtship.

As our wedding date grew near, I began to notice drastic mood swings that I attributed to the stress and strain of our impending wedding. I simply took them in stride, believing that everything would be better once we were married.

However, I was wrong. Much of our honeymoon was spent arguing and fighting. It was at this point in time when I became confused and really concerned...thinking, "What have I gotten myself into this time?"

My confusion was seated in the fact that three quarters of the time I was involved with an extremely warm, caring, giving, loving, and enabling human being. But, where did the stranger come from...what triggered her appearance...what could I do to avoid running into her? I wanted to be with the Holli I loved, and the stranger was a wedge that separated our sense of togetherness.

If you have ever encountered the stranger in a friend and/or loved one, you might recognize some of the wedging characteristics that I have experienced. The stranger I grew to know was irrational, and the worst possible thing I could do was try to reason with the stranger. In her state, reason was a threat. Inevitably, Holli would feel threatened, and she would burst out in hostile fits of uncontrollable rage, often striking (verbally and/or physically) the nearest object or person. The severity of these bouts would also vary which I did not understand. Needless to say, I found it difficult to be close during these unpleasant episodes.

Along with not feeling close with Holli, came other confusing and disturbing feelings about myself. Before I became re-acquainted with the forgiving God that I know today, I believed that I was being punished for divorcing my first wife and for the havoc that it had created in my children's lives. I felt mountains of guilt, shame and responsibility because the things Holli verbally attacked, very often struck at the things that I held dear—friends, family, self-esteem, and my very being. I believed that I was getting what I deserved. But, of course, this got old quickly, and these feelings were replaced with the feeling of resentment.

I recall the deep resentment I felt toward the wedging qualities inherent within the stranger. I hated the divisiveness they would temporarily create in the typically close relationship Holli and I enjoyed. I was also bewildered and sometimes felt betrayed that Holli did not treat other people in the same way in which she treated me during one of her PMS episodes.

One of the most confusing behaviors that I can recall had to do with the stranger-PMS's uncanny ability to transform herself temporarily into Holli when interacting with others. But, when alone with Alexis and me, she would promptly return to her unpredictable self. While being Holli, she used a soft-spoken voice—a tone I would often refer to as her telephone voice. We could be in the midst of our worst confrontation, the telephone would ring, and Holli (not the stranger) would answer. I would ask her, "Why is it, that you are able to treat others so kindly one minute and Alexis and me so miserably the next?"

I do not believe she has ever answered this question, but it is my contention that it was really Holli temporarily over-coming the stranger-PMS's hold. Because appearances are important to Holli, she would use ALL of her human strength to avoid allowing others to see the stranger-PMS. Away from the others and drained of her human resources, the stranger-PMS was given free reign. This was very hurtful, I felt less important and unloved, and at times, I was hopelessly frustrated.

During those pre-help months, my frustrations were many:

- Not knowing nor understanding what was going on around me.
- The shared feeling (with Holli) of being totally out of control.
- Feeling responsible for the changes that would occur in Holli.
- Later, knowing what was going on and still choosing to engage in our potentially-mutual destruction.
- Holli's early denial that anything was wrong.
- My gravest frustration – the wasted time, emotional drain, and the distance created by the debilitating but conquerable stranger-PMS!

At first, in order to cope with these frustrations, I would withdraw my heartfelt feelings for Holli in an effort to avoid pain. However, when the pain did come and was unbearable, I also found myself wanting to utilize this evasive technique to punish Holli. I quickly learned that this punitive approach was the worst possible thing that I could do for either of us. Holli's hurt was amplified a hundred times over, and my guilt was more unbearable than the pain.

Today, I am more aware of Holli's periodic mood swings, and I am quick to verify my perceptions. In the beginning, I was not very tactful nor sensitive when questioning Holli about her condition or state of mind. While looking for the right words to use when asking if what I was perceiving was the onset of PMS, I finally suggested, "Are you feeling like yourself today?", and Holli reinforced that this was an acceptable perception check. It was appropriate wording that would not provoke the stranger-PMS, but rather communicate awareness, concern, and empathy. This mutual check enabled Holli to muster additional strength in her effort(s) to subdue the stranger-PMS. Our most recent perception check is, Are you off key?" Ninety-nine percent of the time, she is honest in her response, thus avoiding what could be an ugly confrontation.

Once aware that the stranger-PMS's shadow is beginning to fall over Holli, I depersonalize myself from the stranger-PMS and focus on Holli's immediate needs: LOVE (in the form of acceptance), tenderness, touch, compassion, and active listening. Along with these come my understanding and support of her need of additional sleep, and my assistance in helping her to comply with her prescribed diet and vitamin supplement.

Each morning, I also jot her a personal note on her napkin which reinforces her self-worth and value. I note my appreciation for all the things she does for Alexis and me each and every day. This timeless piece of communication has made an incredible difference! Our morning prayer time just before leaving the house has made a significant difference—especially during those difficult times! I have also learned that sending flowers to her classroom or posting little stickers around the house saying, "I LOVE YOU!" lifts her spirits tremendously. Oftentimes, a gift such as a new nightgown, a piece of jewelry, or an envelope of money for special luxuries will ease the darkness of a PMS day. Other times, a simple hug, or cuddling, or just holding one another in bed has provided timely reassurance. **I have discovered that when Holli is the LEAST loveable is when she requires the MOST love and attention.** Does this sound familiar?

Helping your partner to get well is one thing—but taking that initial step forward in admitting that help is needed is another issue. There were several critical forces that persuaded Holli to seek outside intervention:

- The concern shown by our mutual friend Pat.
- Holli's personal desire to be well.
- God's promise to answer our prayer for a permanent healing.
- My constant nudging and reassurance that there was a logical/medical reason why these changes were occurring; that Holli was not crazy and that God was not punishing her.
- And, the greatest force of all—Holli's commitment to get well—and in this case—getting well was a choice!

Because PMS varies so greatly in its length, form, and intensity, you will have to be the judge as to whether PMS assistance is needed. It is my opinion that if your life and your family's lives, not to mention your wife's, are being interfered with, that the PMS is robbing any of you of the joy of living (even if it's just for a day or two)—then you would only benefit from implementing the PMS recovery program. It is a choice and one that I can testify is well worth it.

Today, through Holli's perseverance, her doctor's balanced prescriptive program (diet, rest, exercise, and supplementary vitamins), our daughter's patience and understanding, the support of friends and family, and God's special blessing, the stranger-PMS rarely appears at our doorstep. And, when she does, she is easily turned away by a much healthier (physically, emotionally, and spiritually) Holli. I cannot begin to express my respect, appreciation, and admiration for the tenacity Holli has shown in tackling her nemesis, the stranger-PMS, realizing that the battle is daily and that the war may never be won! But for now, I am grateful for each additional minute I have with Holli and for having to spend so little time with the stranger-PMS!

Each day that now passes signals another triumphant step toward Holli's full recovery. Her steps are smaller now because the distance to her goal is much shorter. Holli's road has been and is still lined with peaks and valleys, but the valleys are far and few between. The path that Holli has successfully traveled is a witness to others of the incredible gift of joyful strength bound up in each of us just waiting to burst forth when called upon. Holli has chosen to let go and let God. I am thankful for Holli's perseverance, appreciative of her courage, and strengthened by her faith. The end result has ben the fulfilling rebirth of our marriage, and a more unified and happier family.

In closing, I would like to say that men, and for that matter women, who believe that all of the madness, craziness, moodiness, etc. is a sympathy-driven hoax or an alibi used by girls and women to avoid responsibility for their often bizarre, irrational outbursts are missing a tremendous opportunity. You have the resources available to you to help loved ones and friends (and even yourselves) avoid an empty and dark pit of loneliness and despair. What is there to lose?

Men who have taken the time to read Holli's book have also taken what could be their first step toward allowing for a loved one's recovery—you have shown interest! Interest, in this case, is a reflection of concern and the catalyst for understanding. Once a man begins to understand the stranger-PMS, it is hard for me (a husband and father of two daughters) not to imagine compassion and empathy following close behind. In my sharing, I have revealed what has worked for Holli and me. I am confident that out of your love and commitment, many more equally successful techniques will emerge. There is HOPE and LIGHT when we come to accept that God wants nothing but the best for us and that He is able. We need to just let go long enough to let Him complete the good work that He has begun in ALL of us! Hang in there guys—it is worth it!

# A Relationship
# With
# The Living God

# My Gift From God, My Gift To You

Last but not least, I need to mention one other aspect of my recovery process. A relationship with the Living God was and is essential to my complete well-being. No other person, place, or thing can provide me with the peace of mind and the inner joy that the Lord so uniquely makes available to each of us. I am not cured of PMS, and it doesn't matter to me if I ever am. The Lord is always there for me whether I am having a free PMS day or whether I am struggling. I would like to close with a prayer that I have prayed many times and will continue to pray for the rest of my life. As you read through it, I hope it will comfort you, encourage you, and restore you.

**PMS PRAYER**

Lord Jesus,

Thank you for who you are.
Thank you for dying on the Cross for my sins.
Father, forgive me for my words, thoughts, and
     actions that are not pleasing to you.
Help me to forgive myself—to release any guilt
     and remorse that I carry within.
Invade my mind and body with your spirit and make
     me whole and well.
And, Father, give me the strength to face my
     battles and to fight with a winning heart.
Then use me as your faithful servant, to reach
     out and help others.
Thank you, Lord, for being in my life... for
     putting the pieces of this puzzle in their place.

...God bless you on your continued journey.

# Closing

I have attempted to put down my story in words—for many reasons. Each of them seems important, but there is one that stands out above the rest.

This work has been an opportunity to give back to God just a minute portion of what He has done for me. It is impossible for me to thank Him enough for His faithfulness in my life, but perhaps this story (with the time, effort, and love that went into it) will somehow demonstrate my gift of appreciation.

Just as only God would have it, as I have spent my days telling my story, and thinking that I was doing this for Him, He in turn has richly blessed me. It's just another example of His infinite love.

Another reason for expressing my story is to help other women, in several ways. First, I hope that others can see that it was when I truly gave up my will to God that He was then able to do His work in me. As long as I held the reins to my life, He was not free to steer me in the right direction. Along with giving up my will, I had to trust fully what God had in mind for me. It's often difficult to say, "Ok, God, You have my will," but it is sometimes impossible to say (and mean), "Ok, God, do with my life whatever You see fit." I learned that by giving up control to God, my life was never in better control.

Secondly, it is my hope that any woman suffering from PMS will not have to continue that battle needlessly. Granted, my case was an acute one, and most women do not have to deal with such extremes. However, it is ludicrous for any woman to be robbed of the joy of living, even if it is just for a day or two, or for weeks on end. PMS is not a crutch or an excuse for unacceptable irrational behavior. It is an illness and must be treated as such or it can and will disable a woman, and it can and will erect barriers between a woman and those who love her.

Thirdly, I pray that a woman going through any hardship can

witness through my testimony the faithfulness of God. So many times I asked, "Why...why God?" Today I ask, "God, where do I go from here?" By not questioning His authority, we allow Him to dig down inside us, find the goodness, and do His work. And then we learn not to be complacent with what God has done. I learned the hard way that He is never done—there is always room for growth, improvement, and direction.

I am far from being the godly woman that I hope to be, but I feel that with Christ in my life, I am indeed headed in the right direction. He is the only one who is able to take those days of darkness and turn them into a lifetime of light.

# About The Author

Holli Kenley was born in Ely, Nevada. However, she spent the majority of her childhood, adolescent, and teen years in Stockton, California. Her father, a musician and teacher, and her mother, a registered nurse, raised Holli and three other daughters. Holli graduated from the University of California at Santa Barbara with a bachelor's degree in French and music. She obtained her standard elementary teaching credential from California State University at Sacramento and a secondary credential in English from California State University at San Bernardino. She also has studied at the University of Bordeaux, France and at the University of Upsala, Sweden.

Holli has taught at the middle school level for the past fifteen years. She especially enjoys teaching English and literature to eighth graders as well as being an advisor for the California Junior Scholarship Federation. Her colleagues voted her Teacher of the Year 1990 - 1991.

Holli is actively involved with her church in Palm Desert. She enjoys playing her flute as part of the music ministry, attending women's functions, and participating in home fellowships. Because of her personal involvement with PMS and her desire to help other women, Holli has started her own ministry—Your PMS Friend. By authoring her own book and speaking to audiences on the subject of PMS, she hopes to enlighten women on the subject and to bring joy into their lives. In her spare time, she enjoys spending time with family, entertaining friends, cooking, and writing.

Holli lives with her husband and daughter in a small mountain community in Southern California.

If you would like to write to Holli Kenley regarding your comments or questions about PMS or would like to purchase additional copies of *The PMS Puzzle*, please send your inquiries to:

Your PMS Friend
P.O. Box 12318
Palm Desert, CA  92255-2318

To learn how to control premenstrual syndrome and receive more information, please contact:

**THE PMS CENTER OF CALIFORNIA**
1-(800) 597-2555
OR
**PMS ACCESS / MADISON PHARMACY ASSOCIATES**
1-(800) 558-7046

# References and Recommended Readings

Bender, Stephanie DeGraff, M.A., and Kathleen Kelleher
*PMS: A Positive Program to Gain Control*
Los Angeles, CA: Body Press, 1986

Dalton, Katharina, M.D.
*Once a Month*
Claremont, CA: 1987

Norris, Ronald V., M.D., and Colleen Sullivan
*PMS: Premenstrual Syndrome*
New York: Berkley Press, 1983

This book VALIDATES the illness of PMS—allowing women the peace of mind that they are not the problem or that they are not going crazy...

This book COMFORTS the PMS woman—letting her know that she is not alone in her struggle or suffering...

This book ENABLES the PMS woman—providing tools by which she can enhance the quality of her life...

This book OFFERS hope—giving any woman who is facing any challenge a faithful source of strength and guidance...

*******

*...It is my deepest desire to help other women—to be on the giving end instead of on the receiving one. I pray my book might be a vessel to reach hurting women—not only with PMS but with other challenges as well.*

Holli Kenley